LEGENDARY LESSONS

MORE THAN ONE HUNDRED GOLF TEACHINGS FROM WALTER HAGEN, BOBBY JONES, GRANTLAND RICE, HARRY VARDON, AND MORE

Edited by

CLAUDIA MAZZUCCO

Forewords by Art Spander & Curt Sampson

Skyhorse Publishing

Skyhorse Publishing books may be purchased in bulk at special discounts for sales promotion, corporate gifts, fund-raising, or educational purposes. Special editions can also be created to specifications. For details, contact the Special Sales Department, Skyhorse Publishing, 307 West 36th Street, 11th Floor, New York, NY 10018 or info@skyhorsepublishing.com.

Skyhorse® and Skyhorse Publishing® are registered trademarks of Skyhorse Publishing, Inc.®, a Delaware corporation.

Visit our website at www.skyhorsepublishing.com.

10 9 8 7 6 5 4 3 2 1

Library of Congress Cataloging-in-Publication Data is available on file.

All quoted material in this book, unless otherwise noted, has been published either in *The American Golfer* or *Golf Illustrated* (US), and are reprinted with permission.

Cover design by Brian Peterson
Cover photo credit AP Images

ISBN: 978-1-63450-342-6
Ebook ISBN: 978-1-63450-909-1

Printed in the United States of America

To
STEVEN BLACKBURN
Without whose help the editor
Would have been more
Than normally helpless

Contents

Forewords

Modeling Early American Golf

By Art Spander

The luckiest thing to happen to American golf, the brilliant author and historian Herbert Warren Wind contended, was that its first great hero was an unpretentious ex-caddie like Francis Ouimet.

The game arrived in America in 1743, years before the country even declared its independence, with a shipment of clubs and balls from Scotland to Charleston, South Carolina. The first permanent club, in Yonkers, New York (just north of New York City), was formed in 1888.

But it was not until Ouimet, a 20-year-old amateur who lived across the street from the course, upset the British professionals Harry Vardon and Ted Ray in the 1913 Open at The County Club outside Boston, that the nation truly took notice of the game.

"A person all of America, not just golfing America, could understand," wrote Wind, one of the few non-players inducted into the World Golf Hall of Fame, of Ouimet. "Overnight the non-wealthy American lost his antagonism to golf."

In the next decade the number of golfers in the US rose to 2,000,000 from an estimated 350,000 before Ouimet's triumph. By 1923 golf was a game Americans played better than any other national group in the world. The proof came when at the cessation of World War I, US players, professional and amateur, crossed the Atlantic and won Great Britain's two most important events, the Open Championship and the Amateur.

Success bred success. Young men and women found their heroes and heroines on the fairways, sometimes even in the bunkers. If theories of teaching still were to be perfected and the equipment—hickory shafted clubs—was antiquated by modern standards, players seemed unperturbed.

They used what parochially is labeled "American ingenuity," working to find methods that would prove advantageous. The country had unlimited space and unlimited vision. The thinking was that nothing was impossible, or as the modern Nike advertisement would tell us, "Just do it."

The golf swing itself has always mattered less than the results of the swing, or as the adage proclaims, "It ain't how, it's how many." Beauty is on the scorecard. If Jim Furyk's flying elbow makes critics wince, his numerous victories (including the 2003 US Open) should make them envious.

What the cinema industry learned quickly was what sport always understood: The public is drawn to stars. Ouimet was nobody special until he was somebody unique, until he was an influence on those who knew of victory, including the 20-year-old from Rochester, New York, who tied for fourth at the 1913 Open, Walter Charles Hagen.

The man who would be nicknamed "Sir Walter" and "The Haig" was an athlete who chose golf over baseball and was as flamboyant as Ouimet was restrained and every bit a celebrity. Hagen was the first professional golfer, who made his living exclusively through playing, as opposed to golf professionals who were also running a shop and taking greens fees.

According to his friend and rival Gene Sarazen, as recorded by Al Barkow in *The Golden Era of Golf*, Hagen didn't know a thing about the swing and didn't care. "He was a natural. And a free spirit. Evincing the classic American image of the lone gunslinger riding into the sunset, Hagen took a chance that he could earn enough money in tournaments and exhibitions to pay his way in the world."

If he didn't contribute to ideas of how a stroke should be played—as his strokes on the green were noteworthy—Hagen was reputed for his help in democratizing golf, although he wasn't necessarily the one who alone enabled pros to enter clubhouses.

Hagen addressed the ball with the wide stance of a baseball player at bat, lunged more than swung, and sprayed shots. But his wildness off the tee was more than balanced by his accuracy from other places on a course.

His championship routine was part golfer, part con man. He might show up for an early starting time in a wrinkled tuxedo, as if he had not gone to bed, but in truth Hagen invariably had a good night's sleep and then redressed in the tux.

Sarazen learned his golf in the caddie yard and from Hagen, against whom he played numerous exhibitions, quite profitable in an era when tournament purses were extremely small.

The son of a poor carpenter from Italy, Sarazen was born Eugenio Saracini in Harrison, New York, in 1902. He would say the key to his swing was he hit a ball the way his father hit a nail with a hammer—a short, wristy blow. He once insured his hands for $100,000, a stunt worthy of any Hollywood agent.

As Hagen had done, Sarazen also chose to be a professional golfer and in time would win all four major pro championships, including in 1935 the second Masters ever held when he holed a 4-wood for a double-eagle two on the par-5 15th hole at Augusta National.

It was the shot that would live with Sarazen the rest of his life and with golf forever. Yet he was no less famous for developing the modern wedge, taking what in the 1930s was called a niblick, a 9 iron, and at an angle attaching a flange so the rear part of the club made contact before the leading edge. It helped him win the 1932 British Open, and some say took two strokes off the handicap of every golfer in the game.

Sarazen was mentored by Ouimet, who worked with him on the overlapping, or Vardon grip, in which the little finger of the bottom hand—the right hand of right-handers—overlaps between the forefinger and middle of the top hand. Starting with Francis Ouimet and continuing through Walter Hagen and Gene Sarazen to the present, players in the United States developed their own styles. The game that was created on the other side of the Atlantic became as much a part of America as the Fourth of July.

The Wizard of Oz

By Curt Sampson

Golf instruction through history has been a stew of the bogus and the brilliant, with dashes of originality and insight blended with lots of snake oil and large chunks of baloney. We eat up golf instruction. Whether or not it is good for our games is beside the point. For golf is so lonely and difficult that there is a psychic benefit merely from receiving counsel, regardless of its baloney content. If the advice does not click, we fret that we were inadequate to receive it, not that the advice itself was flawed. In golf the teacher is to the tyro as the Wizard of Oz is to Dorothy.

Golf instruction has not improved with time. Though the photos and drawings here prove that some of the early teachers were clueless, no modern how-to golf writer is more graceful or incisive than two of the pioneers, Horace G. Hutchinson and Sir Walter G. Simpson. As for hands-on teaching, there was simply a lot less of it in the old days, and a lot less was expected of the lesson. Golf was primarily a match-play sport; strategy and psychology were more important than technique.

Many champions found instruction unnecessary. "I learned to play by trial and error," writes Byron Nelson in his autobiography, *How I Played the Game*. "(We) were nearly all self-taught."

"Never had a lesson in my life," Harry Vardon said in *My Golfing Life*.

"Although Stewart Maiden has quite properly been known as my first instructor," wrote Bobby Jones in *Golf Is My Game*, "it is yet true that I never had a formal lesson from him while I was in active competitive play."

Even Jack Burke Jr. and Arnold Palmer, the sons of teaching professionals, are strong believers in self-help.

Then again, you have Jack Nicklaus, Tom Kite, and Nick Faldo, who depended on the intercession of their gifted instructors. But it's a good thing these guys weren't born 150 years ago. Golf instruction hadn't been invented yet.[1]

---

[1] This piece was originally published for the USGA Museum and Library in 2011.

Preface

This book makes no pretense to be anything but a modern edition of what the greatest golfers, whether amateurs or professionals, have thought and said about the game of golf, which ought to be more popular. Its aim will be achieved if it leads those modern golfers who have hardly even heard of Walter Hagen, Walter Travis, and Stewart Maiden to read about them in other books.

The time between world wars (1918–1939) was the most exciting and creative period in the whole history of golf. It was also the most talkative world that you ever saw on earth. When you'd go into the locker room you couldn't hear anything but people arguing. There was a revolution going on, a revolution in their understanding of what it is like to play golf. It may not inaptly be regarded as the period in which a preparation was made for the wider and more organized professional golf of modern times. This was accomplished by the gradual transformation of the British swing of Harry Vardon, as practiced and taught by the Scottish pros who immigrated early in the century. But when we consider the diversity of styles, the fact that in 1920s American golf everybody seemed to have a "theory" on how to play golf correctly, we cannot be surprised that the process of synthesis was incomplete.

There were not just frequent changes in *the theory of how-to-swing-the-club-head-correctly*; the swing had to be reworked constantly in light of new equipment developing, changes in the architecture of courses, bodily-kinesthetic changes, and technical considerations. Apparently nothing was left to do but debate what golf technique should be, if only we could have one. Some teachers, like Ernest Jones and Alex Morrison, had already begun taking issue with the "modern" view of the swing. They argued that—quite contrary to the modern view—our game has absolutely everything to do with our minds. Our brains evolved to allow our minds to control the movements of the eyes, and it is that adjustment of the mind that coordinates the body's movements during the process of a swing.

Therefore it is the paradox of history—the history of golf—that each generation is taught by the champion or guru who explains the game in the simplest terms. Golfers are told to make the clubhead meet the ball in a certain manner and keep the eye on the ball. But if, at the same time, your mind is focused intently upon some bunker just beyond or some water hazard lurking in the vicinity, you happen to be up against one of the steel-shod laws of evolution. As the mind happens to control the movements of the eye, it will immediately shift the eye from the ball to the bunker or hazard. Mind is the controlling factor in golf. Not muscle. The golf club was not just like a fine musical instrument. Harvey Penick used to say that "Percy Boomer and other fine teachers have taught the swing to neophyte women golfers by comparing the leg and body movements to a dance step."

—Claudia Mazzucco

Begin with the Putter

Putting is quite half the game of golf. It is the most important part of the game. As Walter Hagen said, "The ideal way to learn the game is to begin with the putter and work backward to the driver. The beginner would undoubtedly learn a lot faster in this manner and a lot better too." Walter does expressly state that the proper way to start teaching golf is on the putting green. "If you were to take a person who has never had a club in his hand before and place a ball a foot away from the hole and tell him to make the putt, the chances are he would do it. Then gradually lengthen the distance until you had him standing at the edge of the green and you would find that inside of a week he would be a very good putter. Then take up the mashie and teach him how to hit the ball with this club." He seeks to show that "you would soon have him working to perfection in the art of approaching, and all before he had ever hit a ball from the tee." That is Walter's implicit logic. "When he began to use the wooden clubs, he knows that it is absolutely essential in their use to keep the head down and follow-through. He would also know that if he had learned the other shots with the iron clubs, that the club must do the work instead of the body. That is, we will say the club finishes

1

its works in connecting with the ball before the body puts the power into the swing."[2]

"Consistently good putting is perhaps the most difficult part of the game."

—*Walter J. Travis*

IN A LONG PUTT

1. Secure a line to the hole.
2. Keep the body still and the head well over the ball.
3. The ball has to be struck harder (than in a short putt), but the golfer must be moderate in the use of power.
4. Take the club back farther; the force applied will carry it forward more.
5. Less delicacy of touch is required.
6. Place the ball where it cannot be easily missed at the next attempt.

---

[2] "Begin with the Putter, Then Take Up the Mashie, the Brassie." *Golfers Magazine*, May 1922, pp. 31 & 60.

Focus the Mind Like a Carpenter

A carpenter draws a straight line on a board that he wants to cut. Then he cuts the board with his saw along the straight line he drew. While it is possible to oversimplify matters, the secret of successful putting has generally been outlined in this way:

a. Visualize the path the ball has to take, and shut out all the confusion and any conceivable ways in which the putt could be missed.
b. Study the whole line in order to play the shot with the confidence that the ball will travel on its way to the hole, lying dead or possibly actually holing out.
c. Choose some point on that line to putt over.
d. Concentrate on the line and not on the hole.

Actual analysis of the line includes a useful habit— walk from the ball to the hole and back again. C. E. Whitcombe explains that "the line is the most important thing of all. No one will make a good putter who does not work out an actual line. But if you try to keep both the line and hole in your mind at the same moment, you are likely to fall between two stools. Don't be tempted at the last moment to putt more directly for the hole than you have calculated. Your careful examination of the line will all go for nothing."

"Because of the fact that accuracy and delicacy are at a premium, it follows that contrary forces that hinder these are a serious drawback to good putting."

—*Jock Hutchison*

There is a moment when inspiration and confidence come together, Henry Leach believed; if the hesitation is prolonged beyond that moment "the result is inevitably loss of faith, increasing doubt and timidity, and a distorted view of the situation arising from fear of fate." Hitting the ball just hard enough to get up to the hole and no farther can offer a greater challenge. From Glenna Collett Vare's point of view, it would be appropriate not to overemphasize the necessity of *going for* every long putt. She proposes to play the ball inside the radius of a foot around the hole, which she called "the safety zone."

"The long putt is the hardest stroke in the game when a championship is at stake."

—*Gene Sarazen*

The Man from Whom Golf Hid Nothing

By Ed Homsey

Walter J. Travis was one of the great pioneers of golf in North America. He came to the United States from Australia as a young man, became a naturalized American citizen, and did not touch a golf club until the fall of 1896, just a few months before he was 35. He was on a business trip in England when he was taken aback by the news that his friends from the Niantic Social Club of Flushing, New York were forming a golf club. He confessed to a *"mild contempt"* for the game, but, wishing to keep up with his friends, he bought a set of golf clubs for his return to the US. He was relentless in his efforts to, as he said, *"Bring the game into some sort of subjection."* Within a month of *"hitting my first ball,"* Travis won his most cherished trophy, with a first-place finish in the Oakland Golf Club handicap competition. Soon after, he shot a 110, earning him second place in a medal-play event at Van Cortland Park Links. His game improved rapidly in 1897, with his handicap dropping to a 7. With his self-made technique, using a baseball grip, Travis was not a classic swinger of the club.

In 1898 and 1899, Travis firmly established his reputation as a player to be watched, with his narrow defeats in the US Amateur Championship's semifinals. His breakthrough came in 1900 when he earned a hard-fought victory over longtime nemesis, Findlay S. Douglas, for the US Amateur Championship. With this victory, Travis sealed his position as the rising star among American golfers, both as a medalist and match-play competitor. Over the next three years, with his 1900, 1901, and 1903 US Amateur Championships, two Metropolitan Golf Association championships, and a second-place finish in the 1902 US Open, Travis earned acclaim as America's top amateur golfer. His crowning achievement as a golfer came in 1904 when he became the first non-Brit to capture the British Amateur Championship.

Travis dominated the amateur golf scene until his retirement from competitive golf in 1916 at the age of 54. Though a master at match-play, he won innumerable Medalist honors and, in the process, frequently established new course records. His golf résumé included: four MGA championships, three North and South Amateur Championships, and frequent medalist at the US Amateur Championships. Travis was known as an innovator who continually sought ways to improve his game. He installed smaller-diameter cups on the putting green at Garden City Golf Club, his home course, to improve his putting. He was the first to use the new Haskell wound-rubber golf ball to win a major championship, and, at the British Amateur, he used the controversial Schenectady putter. In 1905, *Country Life in America* published a Travis article detailing his experiments with driver shafts that varied from 42 to 52 inches in length.

Travis's influence on the game extended to other players who took note of his unmatched putting skills and understanding of the game. In 1924, Bobby Jones received a putting lesson from Travis that, according to all reports, transformed Jones from an average to outstanding putter. Francis Ouimet credited Travis with *"opening my eyes"* to the importance of *"how I played shots."*[3]

---

3 A large portion of this text was originally published within the article "Kneeling at the Shrine of the Goddess of Golf" at www.TravisSociety.com and is reprinted here with permission of The Walter J. Travis Society.

A Lesson with Walter Travis

By Walter Travis

1. Putting calls for the highest degree of skill and the nicest kind of judgment as regards accuracy and strength.
   Be governed by your first impressions.
2. Let the muscles act upon the information so conveyed without further ado. The subconscious mind is a better putter than the conscious.
3. How to putt with the proper strength is more an instinct than anything else.
4. There is a scope on the green for the play of the subtlest and most intelligent skill.
5. Accuracy is the passage of the ball over an imaginary line between it and the hole.[4]

"Sufficient strength shall be put into the stroke as to ensure the ball reaching the hole with so very little to spare that there shall be no risk of its running far past."

—Walter Travis

---

4 Walter Travis in "How to Putt," *The American Golfer*, March 1911, pp. 367–370.

Q & A

Straight & Strength

Q. According to Walter Travis, what are the two essentials with respect to consistent putting?

A. Writing as always in a popular rather than a technical language, Travis indicates that the two essentials with respect to consistent putting are 1) to secure the ball traveling on a straight line to the hole and 2) The matter of requisite strength. He said, "It is not too much to say that nearly everyone may be taught to putt a ball on a straight line. It is impossible, however, to teach anything in regard to the necessary strength employed in the stroke. That rests entirely with the player himself, and by practice only can any high degree of proficiency be attained."

Q. Which was the best method of putting for Travis?

A. The best method was off the right leg. He did not lay so much stress upon the stance but upon the proper manipulation of the writs and to the "all important fact that in no circumstances the body should be allowed to enter into the stroke at all," he said. Although he had no notion of imposing a new dogma of putting—men putt well in all kinds of different positions—balance was, however, the essential thing. "It is easier to swing a club forward on a straight line with the right wrist than with the left," he added. "The movement of the left wrist is backward and it is infinitely easier to make the club travel on a straight line by means of the right wrist. For this reason, therefore, I strongly favor the employment of the right wrist only in the actual striking of the ball. In taking the club back the initial movement is made by the left wrist. After that the functions of the left hand cease entirely except for the purpose of steadying the club."[5]

Q. What conclusion did Travis draw from Abe Mitchell's description of his swing when he said that his left hand almost "stops" as the right comes to the ball and reaches forward as far as it can during the stroke?
A. How would Mitchell reconcile such conflicting statements? Travis asks himself. For if the left hand almost is "stopped" must not the right hand also be stopped since the speed of both is bound to be about the same? What we shall see is how both hands are dashing into the stroke with apparently the same abandon. When we see how both hands are going through with virtually the same speed, we perceive the stroke not as there being a "sudden stoppage of the left" but as increasing the speed at the moment of impact. Thus the speed at that particular moment is higher than it has been at any time since the downward movement began. Wrote Kerr N. Petrie, "What Mitchell may have meant to convey is that he is pushing harder with the right than he is pulling with the left as the club-head meets the ball, but as for stopping, or almost stopping, the left hand at the moment of impact while the right hand goes on through. It simply can't be done."[6]

5 Material from Q&A 1 and 2 from Walter J. Travis in "How to Putt," *The American Golfer*, March 1911, pp. 367–370.
6 Kerr N. Petrie in *The New York Herald*, March 28, 1920.

Don't Jerk the Putter Back

- It is a great advantage for a system of putting to study the general lay of the land on which the green is situated and the run of the ground between his ball and the hole. Strike, then, the ball accurately.
- Send the club-head through the ball in a smooth manner, enabling the ball to run past the hole in case it does not fall in.
- Stay still, take the club well back from the ball, and do not poke or push at the ball but hit it.
- It is like firing a rifle. A solid, rhythmical contact of club and ball is as essential in the drive as in the putting.

"A fast-moving ball has an annoying way of rimming the cup."
—T. Philip Perkins

- Most golfers tend to put complete trust in their own touch and to assume that they should hole in every putt that is within a foot or so from the cup. That only makes the game tougher for themselves.
- As a general rule, hit the ball sufficiently hard to go not more than six inches past the hole.

What Is "Touch"?

By Vivian Doran

The subtle thing which we call 'touch' is the faculty of feeling the resistance of the club-head as it is swinging towards the ball. Having this *feel*, it is possible to correctly estimate the length of the backswing required for the distance which the ball is to travel. The effect of this ability to feel the swinging of the club-head is exemplified when the ball is hit; there will be an entire absence of vibration of the shaft, and a feeling of solidity in the hit comparable to that felt in a satisfactory drive. In fact the test of "touch" is the existence of this solid feeling in every putt. When this condition exists we are in no doubt as to the amount of force required, since there will be no variation in the distance resulting from the application of this force. When the putting touch is lost it is lost at the top of the stroke. To recover it swing the club back as far as the length of the putt demands, then don't start the stroke; let it start itself. When it has started just hit the ball firmly. The quantity of force to be used has been already determined by the length of the swing back and it is now too late to change. You must get the idea that the club knows infallibly when to start, and will tell you through the sensitiveness of your fingers when to turn on the power. This will guarantee the rhythm of the stroke by ensuring sufficient deliberation at the top. Touch is located at the top of the backswing; it is incorporated in the weight of the club-head, and if I let the club-head start the stroke forward, the touch will be right there when my wrists hit the ball. And it is right there.[7]

---

7 Vivian Doran in "The Putting Touch," *The American Golfer*, December 30, 1922, p. 7.

Diversity: As in Creation, So Too in Putting Styles

Good putting has always been dependent upon the use of fine touch. The problem, of course, is the fellow who gets rounds in 36 putts, but on the greens he takes three putts and on six he has only one. For, according to George Duncan, "there is nothing more annoying than, after you have had a look at your opponent's putt and feel glad it isn't yours, to find that he does hole it. Your shorter one wants a bit of holing after that happens." Duncan suggested that putting can be learned just like everything else. If so, golfers are likely to have more success at gaining courage, confidence, and consistence on the green:

"It all depends upon the pupil and of course upon his instructor," he said. "We hear of putting being an inspiration, that a putter must be born and not made, and various other excuses for bad putters. Inspired putting occurs on one of those days when you win your match about the twelfth hole and, after you have finished, your partner reckons up that you have only had 22 shots with your putter."

Leo Diegel tried a good deal of putters and grips over the years, until he came up with a swinging weight method, used to control the yips in his wrists. He did it with just hands and not wrists. As Johnny Farrell described it, "The pendulum swing is quite simple in its execution; the arms, held close to the body moving gently to and from, the club-head meeting the ball and following-through in the direction of the cup. Through this pendulum swing the player is able to acquire the delicacy of touch, which is very necessary if success is to be obtained."

From the perspective of Bobby Jones, it was, however, a physical impossibility. "I suggest that most of us have taken the idea of a pendulum too literally. A pendulum-like golf club with absolutely true face, swung precisely along the line of the putt, and suspended from a point exactly over the ball furnishes the ideal conception of accurate striking. But so long as human toes stick out in front, and until a golf club turns into a croquet mallet and can be swung backward between the legs, there is little hope that this can be attained."

Henry Longhurst emphasized this assertion in his book *Golf*, explaining that "the pendulum of a clock makes an arc of a circle about a fixed center, and I defy any man to do that with a putter." The ability of the golfer to keep the face of the club vertical and produce a circle with it was, for Henry, the essential element in this method, an element which allows an infinitesimal margin of error in striking the ball. If it is possible that the club-head "could be made to travel without leaving the ground at all," he said, "the margin for error would be infinite. In the ideal hitting position, the face of the club would stay vertical and square to the ball at every point during the swing."

Few people in Leo Diegel's day would have argued with the idea that all the work in putting should be left to the club-head. It was axiomatic—a common-sense tip, as irrefutable as the observed fact that most putters were too light. P. A. Vaile champions his notion that the player was under-clubbed and was called on to exert more muscular energy than was necessary. Thus he emphasizes that unless a player can feel his putting tugging at his right wrist-joint he has not the club best suited for the work he wants to do with it. To Vaile the most astonishing part of Diegel's machine-like putting was that he used his putter from a "pivotal point about halfway down his spine," Vaile said, "thus making his putt purely a body stroke, his hands not entering into the stroke. What muscle he uses to achieve this extraordinary result I leave to the anatomists." This bizarre style of putting, employed by the two-times PGA Champions (1928–1929), had for Vaile only one criticism: "The lie of the putter, the sole of which, instead of being flat on the ground, was cocked up on the toe in order that the shaft could be vertical. His methods simply screamed for a vertical, heavier, dead, upright putter."[8]

Do not underestimate the catching power of the hole. The old adagio of being afraid of the hole is felt above all training.

---

8 "Observations on Diegel's Putting," *Golf Illustrated*, March 1931, pp. 34, 35, & 52.

Sensing the Line

By Willie Park[9]

Putting is largely a matter of confidence. When the player goes up to his ball believing that he can and will hole his putt, he has a much better chance of doing it than if he doubts and is given to anxiety as to what will happen to his ball when it passes over a certain part of the green. In such a state of doubt the more quickly he putts the better; the putt will become more difficult all the time.

- If the putt is played fast the ball naturally travels in a straighter and more direct line.
- The line depends to some extent on the strength applied to the ball.
- There is sometimes more than one road to the hole.
- The ball may be putted into the hole along either line; in such a case the player must use his judgment as to which is the easier or more certain path.

---

9 William Park Jr. in "On Putting," *The American Golfer*, December 1916, pp. 104 & 105.

Renaissance Man

A Match for Anyone

Born in Musselburgh, Scotland, William Park Jr. won the Open Championship twice in 1887 and 1889. He was the son of William Park Sr. who won the Open four times. He coined the aphorism "the man who can putt is a match for anyone" in 1890. In saying this, Park had in mind that his "superlative excellence" in putting which led him to the best that the game of golf can ever reach. In a match with Harry Vardon at North Berwick, Park played "something of a historic shot," which he vividly described: "I was amongst the rock, and from there played a firm left-handed shot to the green, backed it up by holing a four-yard down-hill putt and Vardon missing a two-yard putt on the side of the hill, I won a hole which looked like a certain loss. Vardon, at his zenith, was dormie and finished 2 up on me, and it was by putting I held him."

"The older professionals had to play on the greens, not only as nature made them, but absolutely as nature kept them."
—*William Park Jr.*

Introducing

The Schenectady Putter

When Walter Travis arrived in London three weeks before the 1904 British Amateur Championships, his intention was to spend the last ten or twelve days at Sandwich and the interval at Saint Andrews and North Berwick. He had acquired a lot of new clubs. "I was playing so atrociously at both the latter places," he said, "that I left myself a week only for Sandwich, vainly hoping I might get back in form." When he arrived at Sandwich he was in anything but a "cheerful frame of mind." Rather than run the risk of playing badly at the outset and so, unconsciously, becoming prejudiced against the course, "I simply took out a putting cleek, which I had got at North Berwick, and a few balls and walked around a few holes. The first ball I struck I knew I was on the road to recovery. For the first time in two weeks I could 'feel' the ball. The necessary 'touch' and the resultant 'timing' were there, in such sharp contradistinction to the entire absence of these vitally important essentials previously, that I was at once transported into the golfer's seventh heaven of delight." His putting was still the weak feature. Finally the day before the championship, "Mr. Phillips, of the Apawamis Club, and Rye, a member of our party, suggested I should try his putter, a Schenectady. It seemed to suit me in every way and I decided to stand or fall by it."

With the Schenectady putter, Travis inaugurated the follow-through system of putting. Instead of stopping at impact, the club-head follows through after the ball has been hit on the green, adding smoothness and accuracy to the stroke. According to Harold Hilton, Travis used it so devastatingly that British traditionalists, thinking the Schenectady had magic about it, banned it for 47 years. Hilton said, "After first seeing young Bobby Jones at Merion in his first major championship, Travis said that Jones 'would never improve on his shot-making' because his putting method was faulty. Jones changed his putting method after getting a verbal putting lesson from Walter Travis in 1924. Travis told young Jones to visualize a tack stuck into the back of the ball and drive that tack straight through the ball at impact."[10]

"When I am playing for a championship, I feel like taking it to bed with me."

—Travis on his Schenectady putter

---

10 "The Origin of the Schenectady Putter," written by B. B. H. in *The American Golfer*, March 1911, pp. 371–372.

A Foot-Putt

Let the "error" of missing a short putt die on the spot, and forget about it before reaching the next tee. It is taken for granted that many putts won't always drop for you, but good chipping will improve the law of average. Walter Hagen accepts that: "We all miss those at times but we always make up for it by holing one that we didn't deserve any more than we deserved to fumble a short one. I don't worry about that putt because if I did it might get into my head and then I'd lose my putting touch."

- More putts seem to go in when the balls "die" at the hole than by banging at the back of the hole.
- A dying ball reaching the hole had four doors, while the ball that reaches the hole with any speed had only one door: the precise front.
- Don't expect too much. You can't hole them all.

Harry Vardon joins the debate and redirects it: "I believe that every man has a particular kind of putting method awarded to him by Nature, and when he putts exactly in this way he will do well, and when he departs from his natural system he will miss the long ones and the short putts too. First of all he has to find out this particular method which Nature has assigned for his use."

Putting Tips

- Go for every putt, especially long ones.
- Take a brief but careful survey of the whole green. Slopes are sometimes confusing.
- Never take a "good-bye" look at the hole. Put the club down in front of the ball, take the line, and never look again.
- Take up a natural, solid, and comfortable stance. And think about getting the putter blade squarely into the ball at impact.
- Develop a sense of direction by practicing on your carpet.
- Hit the ball on the line that you think it is the correct one. And with the proper speed. The club-head must follow the line to the hole.
- Good putting is largely a question of judging distance.
- Putt quickly, once the line and strength has been determined.
- Mind over putter is a fundamental for success on the greens.
- Never play a careless putt.

THREE WAYS TO MISS A PUTT QUICKLY
- Allow yourself to agonize over the ball.
- Remain undecided whether to hit the ball hard or easy. Or whether to allow an extra foot for the roll on the green.
- Think of how foolish a thing it would be to miss a short putt, and by so doing destroy your concentration.

"If you have the patience to carry out proper instructions and to practice, putting is surely the easiest thing in golf to learn. The secret of good putting is practice, and practice, and practice."

—*P. A. Vaile*

Never Up, Never In

By Francis Ouimet

In no other branch of the game are all men born so "nearly free and equal." In my putting I take a stance well over the ball, in fact, my head is directly over the ball, and the latter is about midway between the two heels, the stance being fairly open. I have tried putting off the left foot, but found that with this stance there was a tendency to "stab" the ball. Taking the club back, my wrists do not come into play at all, the backward motion starting from the left shoulder and coming back from the right, like a pendulum. It is the right hand which imparts the blow and I endeavor to get a distinct follow-through, with the face of the club-head at absolutely right angles to the hole.

I do not attempt to hold a rigid position, but allow my body to go forward slightly toward the hole. I do not attempt to hit the ball above the centre for a half-top, the stroke which some claim makes the ball hug the ground and be more certain of dropping when it strikes the hole. Rather, my idea is that the follow-through in itself does this work. The club-head, at the finish of the stroke, is between three and four inches from the ground, a result which cannot be attained by a stabbing stroke. To sum it up, my idea is that if the ball were placed on a piece of tape stretched directly toward the hole, the club-head should hold, as nearly as possible, the same position with relation to the tape from the backward motion to the follow-through. It is one of my mottos always to be "up."

My final word of advice would be this: No matter what your putting style may be; no matter whose style you may try to copy; no matter whose advice you may take about putting—practice assiduously.

Suggestions: Generally try to be past the hole, rather than short. It gives more confidence for the next putt. Try to hit the ball squarely and firmly. Do not study the line too long and do not putt carelessly. Practice![11]

True putting philosophy says, Never up, never firmly played.

---

11 Francis Ouimet in "Close to the Flag," *Golf Illustrated*, November 1926, pp. 17 & 45.

Male & Female: A "Dramatic Difference" in Attitude?

This is what I find particularly interesting about the sexes in golf: the different psychological processes, particularly on the green. Galvanized into action men are theoretical, for one thing. They love the putting drama. They need the routine of seeing the stroke from different angles, the calculation of speed, and the mental representation of the line. The ball will never go in if the putter blade is not squarely into the ball at impact, plus they love drama anyway, so the hysteria over a three-foot putt is an inherent aspect of their psyche. On the other hand, women are practical. Putting is, pure and simple, a stroke for them. They are able to judge distance by carefully observing the line and subtle undulations on the grass and they hit the ball without delay. It is not surprising, then, that women are generally good putters, for "delicacy of touch is what is required in putting," according to John Taylor. Glenna Collet Vare, who played golf competitively in the 1920s and won the US Women's Amateur Championship five times, concluded that her mind was simply not focused correctly or that "confidence has left me at the crucial moment when I miss putts of less than three feet. I've never been able to find an adequate excuse for missing those putts."

How to Use Many Putts

(Mistakes You Should Not Make)

By Grantland Rice

- First, in addressing the ball for the first putt, stand over it long enough to get completely rigid, if not jumpy in the nerves.
- Look at the line to the hole and then try to judge the speed of the green and the distance to be covered.
- Think of all these details in one blurred mass as you start your backswing.
- Start the backswing with something approaching a swift jerk.
- Then stab or jab the ball without any attempt at a follow through, lifting your head and moving your body.

This will leave you six or seven feet short of the cup, or five or six beyond. But you will probably be short.

- Missing the next putt is child's play.
- Grip the shaft of the putter as tightly as possible.
- Get completely rigid.
- Use another fast, jerky backswing and once more stab the ball as the body moves.
- This method is sure to leave you another putt of 18 or 20 inches.

BE SURE
- Not to lighten the grip and keep the head and body still.
- Not to start the backswing evenly and smoothly without any hurry.
- Not to stroke the ball on the way through. For in that case you will probably hole out from five or six feet and so miss the pleasure or thrill of taking another putt.

You can always increase the number of your putts by increasing the speed of the putting blade and the tightness of your grip, or by lifting your head and moving your body.[12]

"The line may look different when one takes up the stance. It takes a lot of willpower not to be influenced by the new impression."
—*T. Philip Perkins*

---

12 *The American Golfer*, April 21, 1922.

The Pro Who Shot His Putter Three Times

On May 1942, at a tournament in Orlando, Ky Laffoon produced a pistol from the trunk of his car and proceeded to shoot his putter three times, shouting: "Take that you son-of-a-b—! That's the last time you three-putt on me!" He had such a temper that his fellow pros would give him a wide berth on the course if he missed a makeable one. He began to "blame his tools" and started referring to his putter as "my son-of- a-b—." After one particularly bad day on the greens, he drove 400 miles to the next tournament with his putter tied to the rear bumper of his car. The reason? He wanted to "teach it a lesson." Another tale is told of him running off the green and holding the offending club under the surface of a pond, shouting: "drown, you son-of-a-b—, drown!"[13] He also had the habit of leaning out of moving cars to grind the leading edge of his clubs on the pavement below.

---

13 Quoted from Dr. Milton Wayne in "Ky Laffoon," *HK Golfer*, December 2010.

The Secret of Touch

According to P. A. Vaile, it is centered between the thumb and forefinger of the right hand. "The putter fits up solidly into the angle made by the joint, half-way down the thumb, pressing firmly up against the root joint of the first finger." Vivian Doran located touch at the top of the backswing: "It is incorporated in the weight of the club-head, and if you let the club-head start the stroke forward, the touch will be right there when your wrists hit the ball."

Locked Left Wrist

By Bobby Jones

I believe every teacher will advise that the putter head should finish low. And that can be accomplished only by allowing the left wrist and arm to move forward as the ball is struck. This is the most necessary movement in the whole business of putting. Its omission results in what I call a "locked left wrist" and it may cause almost any sort of error. The remedy is little more firmness in the left hand grip as the ball is struck and don't be afraid to let the arm move with the stroke and so remove itself from the way of the stroke. The very uncertainty attendant upon the success of even the well-hit putts should make us doubly anxious to learn to strike every one truly, for if we cannot be sure of the good ones how can we hope to sink the putts which we actually mishit with the club-head.

"It is easier to putt back to the hole than to continue on the same line with a putt that was previously short. When a golfer has to putt back from the far side of the hole, he has the satisfaction of knowing that he gave the hole a chance."

—*James Braid*

The Art of Being Up

By Walter Hagen

It is wonderful how many 15-, 20-, and 25-foot putts you will drop when you make a habit of getting the ball up as far as the hole. Did you ever stop and think after a round how many putts on the right line stopped from two feet to four inches short of the cup where a little more daring would have saved a stroke? There was a time when from 15 to 20 feet away, I merely tried to set the ball dead. Now I have confidence enough to get the line and give the ball a chance unless I happen to be on very keen or tricky greens.

To develop a good putting stroke, one must learn the putting touch—the most delicate touch in golf, and he must also learn to develop boldness at the same time. The bold putter reaps his reward too, as many balls will obligingly drop into the hole instead of running past. The ball will never drop in if (it is) hit with insufficient strength to go at least hole-high.

"I prefer a fast green because I happen to be the type of golfer whose best touch is with the putter."

—*Walter Hagen*

A Trinity of Games

By Walter Travis

There is no royal road to success. The path is not an easy one, which is one of the chief reasons why golf has such enduring lure. Golf is really a trinity of games: three in one. There is the drive, the approach, and the putt. In the long game, distance and a fair measure of accuracy are the cardinal requirements. The approach calls for regulated strength, plus accuracy of direction for all kinds of distances and from a variety of lies, while the putt is a modified approach combining strength and accuracy in the highest degree, joined to delicacy of touch. Ability in any one of the three departments does not necessarily carry with it skill in the other two. It is the coordination of all three at once and the same time that spells success. A good hole may be likened unto a pyramid laid on its side, the base representing the teeing-ground and the apex the putting-green. The nearer the apex the more the difficulties increase.[14]

---

14 Walter Travis in "Building Up a Game," *The American Golfer*, October 2, 1920, pp. 10 & 21.

Story Time with Grantland Rice

"A short while back at Pinehurst we happened to be playing in a four-ball match with Walter Hagen, or against him, when he missed a two-foot putt on the third green. 'I'll make up for that one,' he said. And for the rest of the round he holed more varieties of putts in an unbroken row than we ever saw before—being only two over even 3's for one stretch of eight holes. Two days later in the North and South Open we counted 12 putts that he holed from distances between four and nine feet, each putt splitting the middle of the cup.

"'And this is the way he has been putting for three months,' remarked Joe Kirkwood, his playing mate. 'There's never been anything like it in the history of golf.'

"When Hagen stands over the ball there is an air of determination and confidence that makes one think he could never miss from a reasonable distance. Unhurried, unflurried, unworried, there is an unbeatable consistency of rhythm on the backswing which shows how perfectly he has the putter under complete control. With the weight forward on the left foot, he has already braced the body with the right, so that development of an immovable body takes care of itself. Hagen believes he can putt. And if he misses one or two fairly short ones he doesn't weaken in this belief. He never lets a few slips get on his nerves."

"In putting, it is delicacy in striking and a happy merging of caution into boldness in the mental attitude that produces the desired effect."

—*Harry Vardon*

The Art of Making Up Your Mind

There is one categorical imperative: Hit the Ball.

- Start your address routine by carefully aiming the clubface at your intended target.
- Join the hands together as one unit.
- Have a feeling of natural balance at the top of the swing.
- With grip and stance properly adjusted, be sure you start your club-head back from the ball correctly.

"The way to start the backswing is to start forward first."
—George Duncan

- You must control the club-head. A good shot is the result of making the club act properly while in contact with the ball.
- You are trying to get maximum distance. The club-head therefore must be travelling at the maximum speed at the instant of impact.
- Concentrate on making the club act properly. If the club acts properly while in contact with the ball, the ball will act properly.

Thinking is good. To think when the swing starts is not.

- You must strike downward from the top of the swing. And this can't be done with any effect, if the balance is out of focus.
- Don't allow your mind to run ahead of what your hands are doing. Once the club-head is in motion the sole remaining idea should be to hit the ball.
- Keep your eye on the ball and don't move your body. Let the club-head do the work and hit through the ball.

"I tell my pupils to start everything at once: hands, club, hips, and shoulders. Take the club back with an easy pivot and bring it down the same way."

—Stewart Maiden

- Do not jerk; start slowly.
- Let the backward movement and the turn of the wrists and forearms start at exactly the same moment.
- Keep the control in the left hand. And don't leave the left side behind. And be careful not to pull the hands in toward the body in coming down.
- Make up your mind as to direction. Decide how hard you are going to hit the ball.
- Now pronate properly, hitting the ball firmly in the back.

"When your grip is as it should be—mainly with the fingers— you almost can think with your fingers. You can subconsciously manipulate the club as your sense of touch and your muscular sense signal that the clubface position must be adjusted."

—Tommy Armour[15]

15 Tommy Armour (1994), *Classic Golf Tips*, Tribune Publications, Orlando, Florida, pp. 2–6.

- Concentrate on a smooth swing with the necessary freedom and wrist action coming into the stroke naturally.
- Do not be afraid to go through with a long, free follow-through. Swing at the ball. Do not jab at it.
- Remember the slogan and say to yourself: "I'm going on through."
- Build the balance on firm feet and let hands, wrists, and fore-arms work unimpeded in a natural way.
- The less you can think about the action of the wrists, the surer you are to do a simple swing. Your wrist will automatically turn over as the left hand and arm swings the club to the right.
- You shall swing in a natural way and the meeting of club and ball will come in its own good time. Walter Hagen intuitively knew this. No matter how technically imperfect his swing may be, he was always able to "sense at every instant in the swing exactly where the club-head is."

A helpful image Travis used was that of the wrists getting into the stroke. If the swing is coming almost wholly from the left arm then the hit is produced from the right. He said, "The hands really work in opposition to each other at the moment of impact between the club-head and the ball. As the ball is struck, the left arm would stop at the wrist for an infinitesimal fraction of a second, accelerating the speed of the club-head."

Such an intuitive and natural way of swinging a club is analogically reflected in the action of throwing a stone with a sling. As Ernest N. Wright observed a century ago:

"The stone is confined in its path by the flexible string and its motion is accelerated by the gradually increasing motion of the hand and arm as the thrower moves it around his head. The path of the stone, as it revolves, lies in a plane, and the useful effort of the thrower is exerted by his hand when it also remains in this plane. If the stone is fairly heavy the arm of the thrower straightens out as the velocity of the stone increases, and the arm itself as well as the hand and the line, travels approximately in the plane the stone describes. Any effort exerted by the thrower at an angle to this plane of motion tends only to disturb the even and uniformly accelerating motion of the stone. Consider now the clubhead as the stone and the shaft as the line, and it will become apparent why it is necessary to make a proper backswing."[16]

He who has lost his simplicity in swinging the club-head becomes unsure in the visualization of his shoots. Uncertainty in the picturing of the shoot is something that does not go along with low scores. T. Philip Perkins explains that "control over the strength of the grip and a club of sufficient weight are useful aids to better judgment."[17]

"You don't have to kill it and you don't have to do something with the club to make it get up—only hit the ball. The club is made to get the ball up and put some backspin on it."

—Stewart Maiden

16 Ernest N. Wright in "An Analysis of the Golf Swing," *The American Golfer*, August 1911, pp. 289–295.

17 T. Philip Perkins in "Simplifying the Judgment of Distance," *Golf Illustrated*, March 1931.

How to Play Golf— A Guide for the **Beginner**

By James Dwight, 1895

For most beginners it would be useless to go out on to the links and to try to go around them without some preliminary practice.

1. Get a professional greenkeeper to give you some lessons (very probably you cannot get such teaching).
2. If not, find the best local player to show you how the strokes are made.
3. Watch him carefully and try to imitate him—probably he will lead you into some bad habits but it is the best you can do.
4. Check his instruction by studying the best books on the game.
5. You must learn to play all the strokes well—each stroke shall be learned more or less by itself.
6. Start with the driving and work at it till you are sure that you can hit the ball 100 yards or so, preferably straight.
7. Don't mix different strokes at first.

There is no use in making one bad drive and then following it with a worse approach shot and so on until eventually you find a hole.[18]

---

18 Dwight, James. *Golf: A Handbook for Beginners*, Overman Wheel Company, New York, 1895.

HENRY LONGHURST ON WALTER HAGEN

"Where other men strove for consistent perfection, it was part of Hagen's philosophy to expect his quota of downright bad shots in every round. So they did not upset him. He was the showman par excellence, the master golfer-entertainer. Life has been very much the richer for having known Hagen."[19]

---

19 Henry Longhurst in 1940, "Who Is Going to Be Second?" *The Best of Henry Longhurst on Golf and Life* (1979), William Collins Sons & Co. UK, pp. 67–72.

As a Bird in Flight

In the 1920s, before the advent of television, the act of swinging a club was still a mystery and a craft. The average golfer could not decipher the swing of Bobby Jones and try to imitate it. Then, in 1938, a new sequence of photos taken by Dr. Harold E. Edgerton of Jones's swing showed that the velocity of his swing increased at the moment of impact while that of the ordinary golfer was falling off at impact. Though he could do it unconsciously, Jones started to accelerate his swing earlier than the average golfer, which is why P. A. Vaile said that Bobby was the only player he ever knew that "finishes his hit before to get to the ball."

Swing the Club-Head

By Ernest Jones

The purpose, of course, is to hit the ball with the club-head, and the club-head is manipulated by the hands alone. Hence it is of prime importance to develop a perfectly clear mental picture of what the hands should do. In a golfing sense, swinging means moving the club-head in a rhythmic manner under control through the sense of feeling in the hands; learning to swing means learning to sense this control, so that you are able to know from the sense of feel whether the movement is a swing.

You should not be using your hands merely to grip the club. You should feel you use your hands to swing the club-head. So then we get to what concentration in a golf swing should be. You must be perfectly clear on what your hands should do, and then concentrate on feeling whether you actually are getting the motion to the club-head with your hands. Most golfers forget it completely in trying to think of the thousand and one tips to help them do that very simple thing. To do this, obviously, we must have control of the head of the club to hit the ball with it.

The action of the club in hitting the ball is to be able to get the maximum distance with the ball; the club-head must be traveling at the maximum pace when it reaches the ball. We must then devise a method that will enable us to cause the club-head to reach its maximum speed as it comes to the ball. Now let me call your attention to the action of a pendulum. At first thought the action of a pendulum does not in the least suggest pace. But a moment of consideration will convince one that there is nothing [that] can travel faster, for if a pendulum should continue its course in one direction, the result would be a complete revolution, and unlimited speed may be developed in revolutionary motion. So then, consider the action of the club as the action of a pendulum.

Obviously once more it is possible to feel what we are doing with the club-head only through the points of contact between ourselves and the club—that is the hands and fingers. If we have control, it means we can feel what we are doing with it. Mostly control is intuitive. For instance, in writing, we feel control of the point of the pen on paper, or in tossing a ball we feel control to throw with the thumb and fingers. Thus we have to feel that we have the sense of moving the club in a pendulum motion, through or by means of the hands and fingers.

You must get the mental picture of hitting with the club-head, just as you have the same mental picture of hitting a nail with the head of a hammer. That must be the start of any golf swing that will ever get you anywhere. It is the first basis of the swing, and it is something few average golfers ever consider at all.[20]

---

20 Ernest Jones in "Hit with the Club-Head," *The American Golfer*, July 1927, pp. 27 & 52.

On the Movement

By James Douglas Edgar[21]

"The manner in which the club-head meets the ball is the essential part of the golf swing. It is in the two or three feet immediately before and after impact where the real business takes place; it is there that the master-stroke is made and the duffer's shot marred, and it is to this fact of the swing I am referring when I speak of the movement. It is not the position of hands, wrists, elbows, body, etc., at the top of the swing that makes the shot, nor is it a wonderful follow-through. The position of body and hands at the top of the swing is a matter of considerable importance, for only an artist can be hopelessly wrong at the top and yet be able to adjust himself in time. For those who have acquired the movement—and all can certainly do so by exercising self-control and by practice—golf is intoxicating. It has the exhilarating effect of champagne, without the after effects."[22]

At the heart of Douglas's game was a mental state that, to him, constituted a feeling of comfort that came when his hands felt "thin." He knew then he was right.

---

21 Editor's Note: The editor has altered the order of the sentences from how they originally appeared, in order to better synthesize James Douglas Edgar's thoughts for the reader.

22 James Douglas Edgar in *The Gate to Golf* (1920), Edgar and Co. England, p. 18.

How to Shoot a Golf Ball Correctly: A Lesson

By Bobby Jones

1. To hit a golf shot correctly the player must move toward the ball, not away from it, as his club gathers speed.
2. At the instant of contact, he must be over the ball where he can perform consistently and accurately the job of hitting.
3. He must be in position to utilize the pull of his left side.
4. He can't expect to get results by standing back and throwing the club at the ball.
5. The left hand should drive straight through the impact position in the effort to direct the head of the club precisely along the line of play.

In a sound golf shot the back of the left hand is visible at the instant of the impact to an observer standing immediately in front of the player.

Seven Resolutions to Improve Your Game

By Walter Hagen

I will always keep my head down: I dare say it will quickly be broken by 99 percent of us. We might also add: "I will keep my eye on the ball," but this goes along with the first resolution. If your head is down, it's an easy job to see the ball.

I will not press: Pressing means usually the fault of getting your body in ahead of your club. Hold the body still until the club-head comes through and hits the ball.

I will follow through: Don't stop your club after it has hit the ball but let it go along in the track of the ball as far as possible.

I will keep my balance: In order to live up to this, don't come up on your toes either at the top of the swing or in the act of hitting the ball. Settle well back on your heels and this will give you a chance to get more leverage in the following through.

I will not put my feet too close together: Many a good golfer has been ruined by a poor stance. Put your feet well apart and you will find it hard to fall off your balance or commit several other faults that are entirely due to this.

I will keep my mind on the play all the time: If you can't take the game seriously you can never hope to get any place.

I will relax: Too many golfers stiffen up when they start to hit the ball, and this causes no end of trouble. The youth gets more distance out of his shots because he is not "so tight" and gets all that is possible into the swing.

Put into effect the coming season these seven golden resolutions and you will be surprised how your game will be benefited.[23]

---

23 Hagen, Walter. "Seven Resolutions," *Golfers Magazine*, January 1924.

His Own Willful Heart

Walter Hagen grew up in the northern city of Rochester, New York, as a son of working-class parents. He was ambidextrous. He played some left-handed shots. He would occasionally carry a left-handed club for such an emergency. Long before the modern era of videos and technology, Walter Hagen's acute mind was at work, challenging or defending the usefulness and practicality of early golf technical theories. He did not theorize about golf; rather he phrased his thoughts in the form of teachings that in effect allows the golfer to be creative in his approach to the game. He emphasized simplicity: his deep suspicions of learning the swing through practice were rooted in the ways in which clever experts could give the player too many things to remember to produce a smooth flowing swing. In 26 years of competitive golf, he worked tirelessly to promote the game and was the first to make a million dollars, traveling around the world, and playing well over 2,500 courses worldwide. He played three different courses in one day. His answer to defeat was also remarkably simple yet incredibly impressive: they will never find him sore or sulking. And if he started out behind they will never find him quitting, for he has pulled too many forlorn hopes out of the blaze. He gave his first British Open Championship's check (about $375) to his caddie. "Hagen has shown that he can win with a smile and lose with a smile," Grantland Rice said, "that he can be in rare good humor when his game is working and in rare good humor when his game is off."

Hagen was the first big-name professional to hold the distinction of being listed in newspaper tournament summaries as "W. C. Hagen unattached." For years, nearly every other competitor was listed by name and club. Oakland Hills in Bloomfield Township, Michigan, was the last club he was "attached" to.

As Walter penned his autobiography, he reflected on the British Course he had played—quite extraordinary, and certainly he found at least three blind holes to one in America. Despite the guidance of a direction flag, he just required a certain amount of guessing at almost every hole, for this flag was of no great help when he happened to be off the line.

The Swing Is Style

By John Duncan Dunn

Swing, in short, is style. Three factors might be mentioned as being necessary for the cultivation of a good style—a knowledge of the principles governing the golfing stroke: (1) observation of the best exponents of the game and (2) an intelligent imitation of their methods; and, thirdly, what has been described in relation to another art as "much exercise of one's own style." This last point is sometimes overlooked. Walter Hagen has a bent left arm at and after the impact. Macdonald Smith has a straight left arm at and after the impact. The man who naturally does either one of these things ought not to change. And it is very observable too that Walter Hagen and Billy Burke have bent left arms at the top of the backswing, so why promote a "pained position" if it is unnecessary.[24]

---

24 John Duncan Dunn in "American and British Thought on Golf," *Golf Illustrated*, November 1932, pp. 20, 21, & 39.

Instructing a Young Golfer

"Do not over-instruct a young golfer. Correct his main faults, but let him work out his own style."

—Stewart Maiden

"An instructor will only be successful in his methods of teaching if he regards each pupil from a separate point of view, as representing a fresh problem both temperamentally and physically, and builds up his game according to the requirements of an individual case."

—Joyce and Roger Wethered

"A good deal of the difficulty in learning golf comes from the fact that the player is often confused by being told to do this and don't do that and so on until the whole thing becomes something of a mystery to him."

—Gene Sarazen

"By the time a player gets good enough to win a number of championships, swinging the club correctly and hitting the ball properly should have become almost automatic."

—Walter Hagen

Control, Balance, and Timing:

The Fundamental Principles of Golf

The Scotch caddie of old correctly appreciated the mechanics of the swing when he said, "Let the club do the work, Let the club come through itself." When P. Fowlie said that the power of the stroke is derived from the acquired momentum of the club that is swung, he once again referred to the intent of sending the ball to the farthest possible distance by swinging the club. It is not a hit:

"When old Bob Martin said that he played 'Like an auld wife cutting hay,' he summed up in six words the whole philosophy of the golf swing. Mutatis mutandis, the movements of an old wife cutting hay are the movements that send Mr. Edward Blackwell's ball some three hundred yards down to the Swilcan burn. Much has been written on the art of propelling a golf-ball, and many have attempted to elucidate the principles of the art, but nothing has been written, or even will be written, that epitomizes it so well as those two phrases: 'Swing like an auld wife cutting hay,' and 'Let the club come through itself.'"[25]

---

25 Fowlie, P. *The Science of Golf: A Study in Movement*, 1922, Methuen & Co. Ltd. London, UK, p. 8.

How to Develop a Sense of Location

By Alex Morrison

This is the most important part of every swing. Without a sense of location, a player cannot hope to properly control and direct the movements of the various parts of his body once his swing gets under way. The golfer must feel what he is doing at all times. This is particularly true of right hand versus left hand domination in the swing. In nearly every case the player could feel, if he would but take the trouble, at the very start of his swing, that his right hand is not only going to overpower his left, but that his left hand holds the club so lightly as to be on the point of letting go altogether.

MORRISON'S PEARLS OF WISDOM

- A good swing is built on sound principles. Self-taught styles are utterly prohibitive of any success in striking the ball.
- To kill one's individuality at the expense of plagiarizing another man's swing too often kills all chances of success.

Send the Club-Head Out

By Glenna Collett Vare

I have the feeling in hitting the ball that I am guiding it toward the hole, though not in any sense pushing it. Maybe I might say that I am trying to send the club-head out straight in the direction of the hole as far as the arms will allow. And, in trying to gauge the hitting, I try to pitch the ball so it will strike a little more than halfway to the hole, to allow for the roll to get the rest of the distance.

How to Make a Correct Stroke

By A. C. Gregson

- To insist too much on keeping the eye on the ball will cramp the follow-through.
- Look at the ball naturally and look at the point you are actually going to hit.
- The head will then take care of itself.
- The club will go no faster than you can swing it properly.
- Any violent body movement will do no other good but spoil the shot.

The club-head must come through ahead of the hands, and both club-head and hands must come through ahead of the body. Swing the arms freely with no interference from the body. In golf anything which sets up tension, anything that is unnatural, is quite harmful.

The Three Golden Maxims

By Ernest Jones

Golfers gain power by knowing the fundamental principles of the golf swing: Control, Balance, and Timing. You must be able to feel how you are swinging the club itself, and your hands—being the point of contact with the club—are the only means of feeling what you are doing with the club itself. That is Control.

The action you are consciously trying to execute is wielding the golf club. All movement to maintain the condition of balance should be purely responsive to this purpose. All balance rests on letting your body give to the action of the club in the easiest manner.

Timing is the art of starting the hit at the right time. It means producing the maximum speed with the club-head at the instant of impact against the ball. It might be defined as the proper coordination of body, arms, and hands to produce this maximum speed at the designated time. This can only be done and felt by the pupil himself through practice.[26]

TIMING A HIT PERFECTLY

Rhythm is a quality of swinging the club-head. At its best it has taken the form of relaxation and smoothness and confidence,

------

26 Jones, Ernest. "Good Golf is Easy, No 6," *The American Golfer*, January 1935, p. 18.

a smooth and gradual application of power that enables one to gradually accelerate the speed of the club-head from the top of the swing down and through the ball, and to drive the ball properly, a freedom that avoids jerky and controlled movements, and produces rhythm no matter how sensitive our innate sense of touch may be. A smooth swing is all that is wanted to send the ball upon its way. To quote Cecil Leitch:

"Perfect timing is everything at golf no matter what shot is being played, and the player who is content to slash at the ball regardless of direction or trajectory will never be a good golfer."

The two ways to develop timing are, 1) Do not hit too soon. Develop the habit of waiting on the stroke, and 2) Think through as well as hit through. A hurried swing is no good for successful golf.[27]

"If the beginner does everything right from the start there would be no use for a golf instructor, but he does not. One lesson at the start is worth dozens later on—because many things are easy to change when the wrong method has not become a habit."
—*John Duncan Dunn*

27 John Duncan Dunn in "Conscious Control and the Lofting Shot," *Golfers Magazine*, March 1920, pp. 17 & 20.

Keep the Eye on the Ball Not a Cardinal Principle

By Bernard Darwin

When it comes to the shorter shots, the eye is quite capable of moving and wandering away. I believe that, in driving, it is possible to harm yourself by looking too hard at the ball. This was brought to me the other day by a personal experience. My driving was not so bad, but I had a thoroughly uncomfortable sensation, as if every time my eye was being forced away from the ball with a jerk just a fraction of a second too soon. The more I tried to see that ball, the more uncomfortable I felt. At last I decided that this confounded eye of mine, the moment it had seen the ball struck, was not to try to stay still or to look at the ground. Rather my head was to turn easily and smoothly round and my eye was to gaze rapturously at the horizon. This seemed a desperate venture, but it succeeded. My follow through was a thing of freedom and joy.[28]

---

28 Bernard Darwin in "The Eye on the Ball," *The American Golfer*, October 6, 1923, p. 19.

Settling the Confusion:

Left or Right Hand?

The champions had no theory or "idea" of how to swing a golf club. What they had was an understanding. Their understanding of the swing was not the result of theoretical enquiry, of a groping in the midst of alternatives about the left-side/right-side controversy and fundamentals of the swing. In 1933, the Bell Syndicate published an article by Bobby Jones entitled, "Left hand of golfer must be dominant." As Jones was a lawyer, it suggested to John Duncan Dunn that he should dispute that statement by "attacking other testimony of the witness." Not surprisingly, the right hand, in Dunn's view, must be dominant because nature intended it to be so. "Try to hit the ball single-handed and you will soon find out," Dunn said.

The apparent disagreement concerning the functions of the two sides of the body is due in great part to the fact that, Bobby Jones said, "Many of the writers on the subject have gained most of their knowledge from observation and the study of pictures. It seems fearfully complicated, this trying to take a swing to pieces and see what makes it tick. These attempts at analysis are quite puzzling enough. But it has been deeply interesting to me to encounter so many times and in so many ways, the factor of body-turn in all shots. After all, the man who does the thing correctly should be best able to tell what forces he himself has set in motion."[29]

---

[29] "Left Hand Control Again!" *Golf Illustrated*, February 1933, pp. 14 & 15.

Use Your Hands

By Phillips B. Thompson

- Swing the club-head with your hands
- Use your hands
- Feel you are swinging with your hands
- In swinging do not resist the natural desire of your body to give with the movement of your hands
- Feel you are swinging the club-head off the end of the shaft
- Keep swinging
- Never let up in your swinging
- You can swing only by using your hands
- If you wish to "swat" a fly you look at the fly. If you expect to hit a golf ball, you must look at it
- When you go wrong, stop thinking and start using your hands to swing the club-head.

The hands are the only part of you in contact with the club. You cannot move the club-head by turning your left shoulder or by bending your left knee.[30]

---

30 Phillips B. Thompson in "Hands and the Club-Head," *Golf Illustrated*, August 1931, p. 48.

A Lesson with Alex J. Morrison

Before his first round the player must learn to picture the swing as a whole. The successful swing is one, full, smooth, flowing motion without mental or physical interruption. Grantland Rice states that this very accurately describes the feeling that every player has when he is at the peak of his game, "when he is able to swing with little or no effort." However, in spite of the thoroughness with which Alex J. Morrison has covered the details of body, arm, and hand action, in many cases, the player seems to be quite unable to execute the swing as it should be made. Morrison observes that this may be the central reason for the average player to hesitate about following them: the very simplicity of the suggestions. "At least I have found it so with my own pupils. When I suggest that they give their entire attention to just one or two points during the swing, they will say to me, 'It's all very well for you to tell us to keep our minds on our chins, but what about our hips, shoulders, elbows, etc.? What should we be doing with them in the meantime?' At the risk of being considered impolite I ignore such questions as long as I can. When forced to, I tell them, as I did at the beginning of their lesson, that, by simply giving their entire attention to the one or two points I stress, they will automatically bring their shoulders, hips and legs into the proper action."[31]

31 Alex J. Morrison in conversation with Grantland Rice, *The American Golfer*, February 1933, pp. 7 and 37.

My Favorite Club

By Walter Hagen

I have in my bag a mashie-iron[32] that has become a pet with me and it has been indeed a good friend in time of need. Perhaps it is a matter of habit that I reach for my mashie-iron when called upon to make a critical shot.

There is seldom a hole that I do not use this club, unless, of course, it is a hole so short that I would be on the green from the tee with my driver or brassie. Frequently I will use the mashie-iron from the tee where the distance will permit me to reach the green with an iron. The range of my mashie-iron is from fifty yards to one hundred and eighty or ninety.

I carry 12 clubs but rarely would I use them all. The golfer, especially the beginner, should learn to use a few clubs well.

In figuring an average round of golf I find that on a championship course with two long holes and others which call for fairly long second shots that I use my clubs about as follows: Driver, 14 times; Brassie, 2 times; Driving Iron, 2 times; Mashie-Iron, 10 times; Mashie Niblick, 6 times; Mashie, 6 times; Niblick, 2 times; midiron, 2 times; putter, 30 times. This totals 74 strokes

---

32 Mashie-iron was a club, corresponding to the modern No. 4, used for approach shots.

and while it varies at times, of course, I have found it to be close to the average.

Golf is a game that is played in the air these days and long low shots are not so desirable unless against the wind. I prefer to play all my shots high as I find no traps up in the air as I often find along the fairway.[33]

33 Walter Hagen in "The Club That Gets There," *The American Golfer*, April 3, 1920, pp. 11 & 38. See also Hagen's autobiography, p. 18.

Start with the
Right Clubs

By John Duncan Dunn

A set of golf clubs should be one harmonious family. They should all have something in common and not be of entirely different natures . . . I would rather recommend to get rid of the discordant club, for it is breaking the rhythm. Likely enough it is throwing you off your game. Sometimes I think it would be a good thing for a man to learn golf without any clubs at all—if such a thing were possible. Certainly his judgment after he has mastered the golf swing would be vastly different from what it was before. Once he has decided to take up golf, he should have someone who knows the game thoroughly pick out his set for him.[34]

---

34 John Duncan Dunn in *Intimate Golf Talks* (1920), G.P. Putnam's Sons, UK.

The Familiar in a Set of Clubs

By Harry Vardon

More than once I have heard amateurs say: "No wonder professionals play so well; they always pick the best clubs." It is not so much a matter of choosing the best—everybody does that—as of selecting those which are in the nature of brothers. The golfer needs what I might call a family group of clubs. The "lie"—that is, the inclination of the club as it is held on the ground in the ordinary position for striking—should be similar in his set in the sense that the full extent of the sole of each club should be capable of resting naturally on the ground when the player is standing ready for the shot.[35]

CHARLES PRICE ON HARRY VARDON

"Harry Vardon was, to state the situation mildly, a hell of a player. For more than 20 years, he dominated competitive golf, not only in his own country but throughout the world—he never threw a tantrum, he never gave an alibi. He just came to play."

---

35 "The Driving Swing," *Golf Illustrated*, November 1921, p. 14.

How to Win with a Swing That Is Falling Apart

By Joyce Wethered

The strain of competitive golf can mean one thing and one thing only, a call upon the tensely-strung nerves. However much a player may apparently be blessed with a calm and placid exterior, appearances are generally deceptive; the odds are that there are a tumult of emotions surging beneath the surface that onlookers rarely suspect. The consolation is that this is an experience common to the majority of those who have to face what's general and erroneously termed, "the music." The music may be felt, if not expressed, when one steps off the last green. But while the ordeal is in progress, the discords are various and numerous. Yet I am certain that no one can excel in any game without having to suffer from the sensations inseparable from nerves.

Overcoming the Snapping Point

By John Henry Taylor

A man is not a machine. Neither can he go on forever. Despite the power of his will and concentration on the matter in hand, the snapping-point must be reached sooner or later, and then it is that the great collapse occurs. Nothing goes right. The golfer is played right out, and nature refuses to be abused any longer. A professional golfer cannot afford to give way to this weakness, so it becomes a desperate fight between determination on the one side and lassitude, caused by over-strain, on the other.

To maintain anything approaching his best form, he must live a clean, wholesome, and sober life. I do not advocate any special method of training. A man must live plainly, but well, and he must be careful of himself. If he uses up the reserve force, or abuses himself in any way, then he has cast his opportunities aside, and he drops immediately out of the game. There are no half-measures. You must do one of two things: Be careful of yourself in everything, or forsake the game altogether. A man who lives a careless or a vicious life can never succeed in golf, or hope to keep his nerves and his stamina.

There is nothing more irritating, to me, than for anyone to come up and begin a conversation while I am engaged in the game. To be successful a golfer must sink his individuality and

69

play the game in an automatic but intelligent manner. You must have the greatest control over your nerves. You must not allow your attention to wander for a moment if you desire to emerge successfully from the ordeal.[36]

---

36 John Taylor in *Taylor on Golf: Impressions, Comments and Hints* (1905), Hutchinson & Co.

How to Develop the Imitative Faculty

By Roger and Joyce Wethered

- The imitative quality is usually stronger between the ages of 12 and 20. During those years the young golfer has certainly a hero whose style and mannerisms he seeks to imitate.
- Allow him to indulge this gift to the fullest extent by affording him/her opportunities of watching the leading players whenever is practicable.
- A young golfer will learn from them by means of incessant copying, the rhythm of the golf swing, the grip, the stance, and everything connected with their methods.
- All the time he is playing shots of his own but is firmly convinced that he is reproducing the stroke of others.
- By a faithful admiration of his hero and the inevitable imitation of him, he may acquire an identical style.

The young golfer should be left to his own resources. His individual golfing character will soon assert itself.

- When he has survived this life of youthful experiments, he will come into his own at about the age of 18 or 20. Mere imitation yields to the exercise of the critical faculty.

From that time onwards he loses the power to imitate and gathers his knowledge in a new capacity of being able at last to detect method.[37]

"The playing of golf is an art, and just as art is a matter that closely concerns the individual, so it is necessary for everyone to discover the nature of their own faults."

—Joyce and Roger Wethered

---

37 Roger Wethered in Chapter III, Instructional, Young *Boy, Golf From Two Sides*, pp. 24–51.

The Great Lady

All her life Joyce Wethered felt a sense of glory in the proud record of her career. She took every opportunity to remind her readers they have to cultivate a natural swing and there is none better than a natural swing. She usually endured the weakness and diversity of golfing "theories" with equanimity, and sometimes she would even joke about it. Golfers deceive themselves and build their games on little white lies. She argued that golfing tips can be used for many purposes: "They have gained a somewhat unenviable reputation for being often extravagant and freakish ideas that are disconnected and do us more harm than good." And they can't be taken in the abstract, but only in a particular situation. She could reasonably say to have never learned about golf by reading technical articles:

"Tips and pure wordy lessons slip out of memory unless they are linked to particular situations on the course. They work a temporary benefit by increasing the concentration of the player on what he is doing, but they will almost inevitably take their revenge by introducing too many isolated ideas to think about at the same time. If you are wise, you will come down to earth as soon as you can and begin to wonder why an idea is working so successfully. You will never discover the reason unless you know already the fundamental idea of the golf swing and are familiar with the first principle of swinging the club."[38]

"When I was quite young I asked my brother Roger how to play a certain shot. 'Oh, it's no use telling you anything,' he replied. 'You will never be any good until you find out for yourself.'"

—*Joyce Wethered*

---

38 Joyce Wethered in *Golf from Two Sides*, with Roger Wethered (1922), Longmans, Green & Co., London, UK, pp. 10–14.

Mindfulness

By Joyce Wethered

The practice of golf appropriately involves a focus on experience. What should be known on the mechanism of the game requires lucid explanation. Their application, however, should be largely self-taught. Experience, in golf or otherwise, is difficult to define. By definition, experience is subjective and, as such, incommunicable. Prior to the mid-twentieth century, the game of women was differently constructed so as to indicate a golf that was plain, and which does not lead to any attempt of advanced iron shots. A look of astonishment was common on the face of a gentleman whose "mixed" partner has pitched over a high mound and laid the ball in the neighborhood of the hole. To solve some of the mysteries of golf was regarded as beyond their reach and as belonging more particularly to the men's own peculiar province. Joyce Wethered added that "the art of pitching was not supposed to exist in the repertoire of a lady. A number of prejudices of this sort are, after all, only superstitions. And there is no need for women to be afraid of thinking for themselves as to the type of golf they shall play or what implements they shall use in the art of striking the ball."[39]

---

39 Joyce Wethered in *Golf from Two Sides*, with Roger Wethered (1922), Longmans, Green & Co., London, UK, pp. 10–14.

"The male margin, mainly through physical power, is still at least nine strokes per round."

—*Grantland Rice*

Lessons from Saint Andrews

- The hazards on all of these seaside links are natural.
- You must drive straight and far.
- Unless you drive into the fairway, you will certainly meet with awkward stances. The ball will be lying away from you or gazing at you from an elevation.
- You must make the ball rise very quickly from an abrupt ridge or mound.
- Concentrate on keeping the ball out of the gorse bushes, which are tough little spiky shrubs that hold the ball with bulldog tenacity.
- Distance is secondary to accuracy.
- The wind will grab a ball and carry it in any direction.
- To execute control over the pitch to the green is the most important factor to win the British Open.
- The greens are to be played as nearly in the natural state as possible. They are not to be artificially altered.

The results all depend on how you can successfully master strange weather conditions.

HENRY LEACH ON SAINT ANDREWS

"One of the most remarkable things I've seen in golf was at an Open Championship in Saint Andrews. By the side of the 18th green, I saw four of the greatest players of this time come up to it in the competition one by one and have putts of less than 18 inches at that hole. Three of the four missed! In the old days, when the greens were not quite as they are now, but became very glassy and slippery with much wind and constant play upon them, I believe there were more short putts missed on the old course at Saint Andrews than on any other two courses in the world, and the task of holing the little stupid golfer on that home green was a most tormenting ordeal."[40]

---

40 Henry Leach in *The Happy Golfer* (1914), MacMillan and Co., London, UK, p. 57.

Hit the Pitch & Chip Shots Briskly

Any chip shot, if properly hit, should result in a one-putt green. The pitch offers a wide range of creative or imaginative options. Rarely will you find two problems exactly the same. It is a shot where golfers can have a choice in creating the options. Bobby Jones points out:"Good chipping is largely a matter of mechanical skill, aided of course by a superior sense of touch and the ability to appraise a slope. The game cannot be played mechanically. And above all one must know what one can or cannot do."

- The pitch is the most valuable stroke in golf.
- It must be executed with authority. Power is not at stake; it is to be played purely for accuracy's sake.
- When you come to a fast, well-guarded green, you can pitch boldly over a trap right up to the cup without fear of running over into another trap.
- If the ball runs over two feet after it lands, you have not played the stroke correctly.
- Try to reduce the chances of landing in a hazard by either aiming for the pin itself or some point whereby the ball won't be too far away from the cup.

"The shot must be exactly timed. If the hands get in too much ahead of the stroke, not even turning in the club face will be sufficient to save the shot."

—*Jock Hutchison*

- Don't play a shot with an unsettled mind. It will introduce, consciously or unconsciously, a movement that is undesirable.
- Devote a little time to practice, both by yourself and under the supervision of a professional. This is the main difference between the golfer who scores under 90 and the one who plays over a 100.
- Shots of 40 or 50 yards and less should have their share of attention. Done properly they should lead to good experiences around the golf course.

"The golfer who is able to put the ball within a 14- to 17-foot radius of the cup by virtue of excellent iron shots is certain to have an advantage over his less skilled opponents."

—*Gene Sarazen*

The Creative Approach

Teach golf neither setting boundaries nor laying down rigid principles.

- Creativity is not the province of a few select champions who can get away with breaking the mold because they possess this wonderful gift of sensibility. It is a capacity inherent to varying degrees in virtually all sportsmen.
- A champion is in a sense more creative around the green than the average golfer, not because they can visualize more possibilities than we can imagine but because they try to attack the hole logically.

"Creativity is favored by an intellect that has been enriched with diverse experiences and perspectives."
—Psychologist Dean Keith Simonton

- Sensibility is in fact work.
- The creative golfer is built on discipline and focus.

"That's like practicing scales on a piano before playing Chopin. In golf everybody wants to play Chopin first and take up the scales later."

—*O. B. Keeler*

Hit Past the Pin

By Harold Hilton

Be up. Do not fail to strike the ball sufficiently hard to make it travel as far as the hole is situated. It is the gospel of "Be Up, Be Up, Be Up," at any cost. I've been preaching this gospel for 20 years and more, and then when the time arrives to apply it to my own game I find that I am a most errant sinner. I can't make up my mind to give the ball that little bit of extra physical persuasion which will call for the putt to be played from the other side of the hole. There are infinitely more strokes thrown away through the failing of being short than through being past the pin. Of course it stands to reason that more shots will finish short than past, seeing that there are invariably a certain number of approaches which are not struck quite cleanly and will not usually travel the requisite distance.[41]

HENRY LEACH ON HAROLD HILTON

"Of Mr. Hilton's marvelous skill, especially on the scientific side, as one might say, there can be no doubt. If it has been equaled among Amateurs it has had no superior. I do not think any man has ever associated cause and effect in golf so thoroughly and

---

41 Harold Hilton in "Be Up," *The American Golfer*, January 1926, pp. 17 & 38.

soundly as he has done. There are very many players who can produce seemingly perfect results with their strokes, but the proportion who know exactly how they produced them, and, more than that how precisely to make the nicest variations in those results, is extremely small. Being the scientific player that he is, and such a master of wooden clubs, he has not arrived at any features of his style and methods without deep thought and a vast amount of experiment."[42]

42 Henry Leach in "The Scientific Hilton," *The American Golfer*, December 1916, pp. 86 & 103.

"Eye for Country"

Regardless of our golfing talent, we are sure to believe that we have benefited immeasurably more by playing golf than we could from any book about the golf swing. Observation of the variety of strokes to be played with a mashie (iron-5 today) and a mashie niblick leads Roger Wethered to conclude that the "eye for country," more than any other element, determines the choice in a given situation:

"The match-winning quality is a combination of two things: the ability to pitch, and to hole the short putt. The value of the former lies not so much in the ability to pull the ball up quickly after it has pitched, as to allow intervening and detrimental influences short of the green to be disregarded, so that the ball may come to earth upon a smooth alighting place (best of all upon the green itself) and proceed unimpeded up to the hole side. The object of the chip is to put the ball dead, or so near the pin that the putt would be holed three times out of four. It is mainly a wrist shot with a mashie. The arms should barely move in the upswing; and the wrists should be the hinge which allows the club to move backwards, although the hands will move forward after the ball is hit. The degree of drag applied by hitting the ball downwards will render its run more controllable."[43]

---

43 Roger Wethered in "The Secret of Short Mashie Approaches," *Golf Illustrated*, June 1922, pp. 12 & 13.

No shot is more soul-satisfying as the approach that comes to rest almost on the brink of the hole. George Duncan assigned an unequivocal importance to this shot, but the reason why many players do not attain great proficiency at approaching is due, Duncan thought, to "a failure to take into consideration the particular circumstances in which each shot has to be accomplished." When you are between 50 and 100 yards from the pin, you should consider which side of the green will allow for an easier putt. If you are in doubt, it is simply a choice of the stronger club. Each golfer knows which club to choose according to his own ability, means, or power. So if you hesitate between wooden and iron clubs, use an iron. Between two different irons, use the one you do not have to force. Yet, at the same time, the ball must get in with as little loss of time as possible. Turning his attention to slopes in the green, James Braid indicated:

"It might happen that the putting is very much easier from one side than it is straightforward, and that on one particular side it is easier from the other. If there is an appreciable slope of the green in any direction, it is easier to put up it than down it. When the hole is in a corner of the green or very close to uneven or rough ground, it is obviously the safe game to play to the other side."

"Remember that complete control of nerves, club, and situation is never actually attained."

—*Charles "Chick" Evans Jr.*

Darwinian Perspectives

By Bernard Darwin

One of the dangers of thinking too hard and too long about a particular system is that we come to depend on it too completely and when, as is inevitable, we miss, we accept this as evidence of the failure of the system. It does not occur to us that it may have happened because we violated some elementary principle. It is not the fault of the system that we swing too fast or take our eye off of the ball. And, after all, we must miss occasionally for no definite reason except that we are human. When we are playing well and confidently, we accept an occasional miss as proceeding from that cause and think no more of it.[44]

---

44 Bernard Darwin in "To Think or Not to Think," *The American Golfer*, December 13, 1924, pp. 9 & 30.

The Old Man Par Idea

The only son of Colonel Robert P. Jones, a prominent Atlanta lawyer, and his wife Clara, Bobby was such a sickly child that he was unable to eat solid food until he was five years old. When in 1908 his family moved to a summer home near the East Lake Club, he grew stronger but there was virtually no engagement with golf. "I liked baseball much better," he wrote, but in the absence of boys in the neighborhood with whom to play baseball, he eventually joined his parents at the golf club, beginning to play a few shots per hole with his first club, a cut-down second-hand cleek. Now that he had some sense of the game, he played to defeat his good friend Perry Adair. But he began to forget about Adair and concentrate only on his score. Bobby felt that it was an awful effort to play the par in those years. And even worse was to come when he entered his first major championship in 1916. In the spring of 1915, after seeing Jones violently breaking down his club after a bad shot, former US Open Champion Alex Smith said: "It's a shame that he'll never make a golfer. Too much temper." Jones did not know what to make of this enigmatic prophecy.

He really had not changed after the First World War. During his lowest point as a player at the 1921 British Open at the Old Course in Saint Andrews, Grantland Rice said that Jones had the "face of an angel and the temper of a timber wolf." That year,

Willie Hunter beat him at Saint Louis during the US Amateur Championship. According to the popular theory, he would define his temperament as choleric-sanguine, sometimes with a touch of melancholy, but without any phlegm. Time and again over all these year, to his great despair, Jones would hear from his playmates and club friends, "You are a great golfer—a great shot-maker. But you can't win. You haven't the championship complex."

To have lived through such a period was obviously draining—one senses that Bobby was sometimes on the verge of a break-down. He reflected for a long time whether the main difference in his game between 1923 and 1930 and the seven lean years when he couldn't win a major championship was the result of a persistent endeavor to save a stroke *per* round: "You are not playing a human adversary. It is Old Man Par and you, match or medal. A splendid fellow when you get acquainted with him. It is the imperturbable economist! Make a friend and constant foe of him, and the other boys won't be so rough on you. Sometimes beginners think, and they're quite justified in so doing, that his friendship is hard to make. It is. And, what is more, it is hard to keep, unless, that is, the players themselves merit it. Old Man Par is a patient soul, who never shoots a birdie and never incurs a buzzard. And if you would travel the long route with him, you must be patient too."

If you extend Jones's figurative speech, we might say that our opponent has nothing to do with our game. It is thus a game against the par. He truly practiced this mantra during the 1923 US Amateur Championship. One of his defeated opponents was Francis Ouimet: "It was a ruinous game for me, because it was just like a human being trying to butt his way through a concrete wall. In neither case could the individual make any forward progress. This is the hardest kind of golf to beat: the kind where your opponent is reeling off par, hole after hole."

Jones enjoyed the greatest prestige and popularity among golfers, pro and amateurs, at the Open Championship as also in America. Of great interest for the British pro was his long and encompassed swing. We see, then, how swinging the club up quietly, and allowing it to go its full distance to the very end, are linked so as to provide great accuracy. His brilliant performance at the qualifying rounds at Sunningdale and the finals at Saint Annes was the subject of a considerable amount of commentary. John Taylor's praise read as follows: "(Jones) compelled the admiration of all who admire genius in whatever medium it is presented, but when this genius is shown with such simplicity, charm, and gentlemanliness, it enhances the virtue as it certainly sheds a greater luster on those who provide it."

Between 1923 and 1930, Bobby Jones entered twenty major championships and won thirteen of them, culminating with the Grand Slam—the 1930 British Amateur, British Open, US Open, and US Amateur. He got degrees from Harvard (literature), Georgia Tech (engineering), and attended law school at Emory, which he left early to take and pass the bar. He retired from championship golf at 28 and went on to practice law. He founded and helped design Augusta National. As Grantland Rice wrote: "The start of Bobby Jones' career to date is one of the most interesting episodes in all sport, one of the most unusual of all careers. Back of this amazing skill there have also been character, magnetism, courage, and intelligence of a high order."

The Secret of Bobby Jones

By James Francis Burke

1. He has studied the use and mastered the secret of every club.
2. He has studied himself and has become his own master, mentally and physically.
3. He has studied and mastered the rules of golf, knowing that no one can play the game who is ignorant of the rules that govern it.
4. He has studied and mastered the etiquette and courtesy of the course, knowing that those who disregard them are the pests of American outdoor life.
5. He is goodnatured in defeat and modest in the hour of victory, an ideal sportsman and a genuine American gentleman.[45]

---

45 James Francis Burke in "Our Bobby," *Golf Illustrated*, August 1926, p. 22.

Judging Distance without a Caddie or a Yardage Book

(And Maybe with Your Eyes Closed)

Harry Vardon had the most perfect judgment in regard to distance. This skill so impressed Hagen, who observed his game at the 19th US Open in 1913, that he did set out to take notes of the distance by sight and stored the impression away in the mind. The sense of touch is later attuned to this impression.

Perkins said of judging distance: "We regard as the most fatal error in golf to change your mind while engaging in the stroke. Golfers must be perfectly honest with themselves in regard to the way the ball is struck. Do not excuse yourself for misjudging a distance when actually you did not hit the ball quite as intended."

Francis Ouimet intuitively grasped that distance is not registered in the mind in terms of feet and inches. He is inclined to minimize the risk of three putts by gaining an accurate judgment of distance and direction. When he actually did this, "something almost magical happened in the green," he said. "First of all, your judgment of distance must be accurate. If you are 30 feet from the hole, you must not putt your ball 40 feet and neither must you putt it 20 feet. You must get it close enough so that your next putt will be easy. Then your direction must be considered as no small part of the operation."

The Quest for Absolute Accuracy

By Francis Ouimet

It is much easier to play a pitch to a green surrounded with trouble than people think. The traps in front serve as a guide with which to gauge the distance and with the flag as the target the objective seems to me to be more simplified than if nothing was in the way and the green was unprotected. I prefer the high pitch to the tightly trapped green, for it is only a matter of getting the correct distance. The shot can be played one of two ways.

1. You can hit the ball straight for the pin, depending upon the back-spin you've imparted to keep it from running very far after it has landed.
2. You can draw the blade of your club-head slightly across the ball at the moment of impact, which produces the shot known to golfers as the cut shot.

Both shots have merit and equal value, unless of course the wind must be considered. The cut shot has a drift from the left to right and in a wind it is not always wise to play a ball that will eventually depend upon the mercy of the breeze.[46]

---

46 Francis Ouimet in "Close to the Flag," *Golf Illustrated*, November 1926, pp. 17 & 45.

Think Nothing at All

By Bobby Cruickshank

On the last hole at Inwood when I was successful enough to get into a tie with Bobby Jones for the national title (1923), I made up my mind on *that* iron shot to the green that it was to be everything or nothing. I pushed everything out of my mind, except the flag on the green and the hitting of the ball. The shot came off all right. But it might have ended disastrously had I not made up my mind that I would not allow anything to disturb me mentally. In hitting the ball it does not pay to allow the little white sphere to annoy you. What I mean is one must not look too rigidly at the ball, as this too is apt to affect one's nerves.

In playing over a pond, ditch, or bunker, you must think only of hitting the ball. The stroke should be a sharply decisive one. Give the ball a good keen rap, by employing your forearms to whip the club-head through. Which will give you extra distance, and it is a mark of first-class iron play wherever you happen to see it.

"The sum and substance for lowering your handicap and improving your game is to PLAY SAFE."

—*Henry Cotton*

- We must be reasonable in all decisions and look for the nearest thing to a safe recovery, even if we cannot win the match.
- Always think of the possible consequences of error. Why would you want to lose two or three strokes if a fine recovery does not come off?
- To get a ball out of a heavy lie, beef, brawn, and muscle are the prime requisites. Without these attributes all the skill in the world will avail little.

"There is a reasonable margin between taking risks and running in a fool-hardy way into sure destruction."

—Jock Hutchison

- It is highly important to know what is ahead before you shoot.
- If you've made a decision respecting the club to use and shot to play, you must then hit cleanly and decisively through the ball.[47]

SUBCONSCIOUS MIND: The mind that rarely makes a mistake. If this proposition is applied to the stroking of a golf ball, it certainly will make no mistakes in directing a purely mechanical action, such as we achieve just the result that our physical ability, eyes and muscle-training entitle us: "Excitement, depression, elation, any emotion could destroy you," said Aubrey Boomer. He adopted and extended this view of replacing the conscious process of thinking. "Otherwise you are at the mercy of your mental state."

---

47 Bobby Cruickshank in "Playing the Long Iron," *The American Golfer*, September 8, 1923, pp. 11 & 40.

Putting Is an Art

Approaching Is a Science

Inspiration does not exist for its own sake. It has its roots in the mechanisms for swinging the club. As Charles Evans wrote, "golf is really a mental problem with a physical solution." He put the pursuit of perfection in striving to strike the ball smoothly and firmly, and neither accuracy nor timing is achievable without the other.

- Upon the hands rests the actual task of placing the ball on the spot where it is intended to pitch.

"The grip of one's club is a matter of personal feeling. It should be grasped naturally with confidence and comfort."
—Charles "Chick" Evans Jr.

- Do not swing back loosely. Bring the club back decisively.

"Any half-hearted methods will prove fatal. At the top of the swing the hands should not have risen as high as the level of the shoulders, and the length of the swing will entirely depend on the bend of the left wrist. With the fingers of the right hand force the blade of the club beneath the ball and push it through firmly, keeping the face of the club square all the time."

—Roger Wethered

Two Wrongs Never Make a Right

By Gene Sarazen

When the Wilson Sporting Goods people ask me to size up a young player, there are two factors which always get my first consideration. One is the hands. The other is the top of the swing, to see if hands and club-head are properly related. Once these two factors have been developed correctly, the player—so far as the physical angle is concerned—has a golfing future. This is because the character of the man's game is built around his hands. His body and all other components respond to the hands. If a player starts off with a faulty grip, I would say that he will spend the rest of his days trying to compensate for it with theories that will do him no good. It is merely a matter of two wrongs never making a right.[48]

PETER ALLIS ON GENE SARAZEN

"Although he wasn't the youngest man ever to win the US Open, he became the youngest player ever to win the PGA Championship. Suddenly, Sarazen was elevated to the upper echelons of golfing royalty; Hagen, Jones, and Sarazen—perhaps the first Americans to be called the 'big three.'"[49]

---

48 Gene Sarazen in "Golf Medicine from Master Doctors," *The American Golfer*, October 20, 1923, p. 22.

49 Peter Alliss in *Peter Alliss' Golf Heroes* (2002) Virgin Books, London, UK, pp. 126–130.

Saraceni
Wins the PGA

In 1923, Gene Sarazen won, for the second consecutive year, the PGA Championship at the Pelham Country Club. On every round he drove straight to the green at the 274-yard 18th hole. He was the only man in the tournament able to drive to the green on the 294-yard 9th hole and the only one to cut the corner over the houses and trees that made the 310-yard 2nd hole a dog-leg. Grantland Rice wrote:

"One secret of match play greatness is to remain serene and unworried in the face of an unexpected rally, to continue playing golf regardless of situation or circumstance to the closing putt. Gene Sarazen's closing round against Hagen called for even harder battling. These two had met in three previous match play tests. Sarazen had beaten Hagen last fall over the 72-hole route at Oakmont and Westchester Biltmore and over the 36-hole route at Asbury. Hagen had an 18-hole decision against Sarazen abroad. Here was Hagen's chance to square the count and Sarazen's chance to make the lead undisputed.

"Throughout the forenoon they played each other in place of playing golf. They were all square with two 78's. But in the afternoon Sarazen went to it. He was slashing his way to the green with a drive and brassie on all the long holes, holes from 500 to 530 yards away. His wooden play was so consistent, his iron play so well timed and his putting so deadly that standing on the 16th tee he was 4 up on par and 2 up on Hagen, who in spite of a stymie and this relentless pace had hung on well.

"Then with victory in sight Sarazen slipped, skidded, lost two holes and found himself all square on the 36th tee. For the ninth time in succession that week he caught the green over the hill, 274 yards beyond the dip. To reach a green nine successive times that is 274 yards away with the narrowest possible approach is proof of superb control.

"A half stymie stopped him here, but to show his determined grip upon destiny he had enough left for a rally to beat par the next two holes in succession, closing out the engagement with a scalp-lifting mashie niblick pitch from the heavy rough to within two feet of the cup.

"Small wonder Hagen buckled up against this charge. Hagen had his chance after a smashing drive, far and true, but the strain had worn him down and that last Sarazen recovery had ended the march. His short pitch to clear a narrow trap failed and for the second year in succession Sarazen was professional match play king of the United States in one of the finest championships and one of the most thrilling yet held."

Q & A

The Inimitable Gene

Q. How many superstitions did Gene Sarazen manage to collect?
A. At least four well known superstitions. 1) Gene invariably picked a red necktie adorned with a large provocative question mark. He regarded the tie as a mascot only to be worn under special circumstances. The charm worked at Fresh Meadow, where Gene won the 1932 US Open with an incredible 66 in the last round. Before each shot he glanced down at the question mark as though thinking: "Here's your answer!" 2) He had a "Tuesday taboo." He thought it bad luck to reach the scene of a tournament on Tuesday and would inconvenience himself to avoid this "curse." In 1922 Gene hopped off a Jacksonville-bound train at Tallahassee and stopped over a day so that he might escape a Tuesday arrival. This fear was a legacy from his dad who once suffered a severe injury on Tuesday. 3) He went into the habit of changing to a new ball after a sloppy hole. And 4) although he was a devoted and attentive husband, he thought his wife was a "hoodoo" in the gallery. Mary Sarazen either sat in the clubhouse or followed her husband at a discrete distance.

Q. Is a golfer more susceptible to the vagaries of fortune than other athletes? Can a golfer make his own luck?
A. Wrote Bobby Jones: "Nobody wins an Open Championship unless the ball rolls for him. The tennis player, for instance, can

100

make his own luck via forcing shots, but the golfer is playing a kind of outdoor solitaire against an invisible foe. He is battling nature as well as flesh and blood rivals. I've won some tournaments when I was half missing my shots and lost others when I was hitting the ball cleanly."

Imagination as an Obstacle

By Henry Longhurst

Golf, perhaps through its very slowness, can reach the most extraordinary heights of tenseness and drama. There are the imaginative golfers who are exceedingly skillful in envisaging all the horrid possibilities attached to every shot, but very bad at executing the intended stroke; for the game of these golfers is destitute of all balance and of all real enjoyment. They are not likely to stand the strain of modern competitive golf so well as one who can proceed serenely on his way, treating (like Harry Vardon) an Open Championship as part of his daily job. I encourage the golfer not to visualize hazards that don't exist, and don't allow first impressions to mislead their judgment.

Imagination is insidiously self-destructive.
- The power of imagination could enlarge small obstacles so as to fill our minds with a fantastic estimative.
- Don't allow difficulties to assume unreasonable proportions.
- Try not to get paralyzed by indecision. If you turn toward your caddie seeking advice, you have weakened your own independence of thought.
- Proceed serenely in your way.

The key to turning imagination into golf is acting as if the visualized shot was already accomplished.

1. Decide in advance what club you think the occasion requires.
2. Take your stance and choke off all element of doubt.
3. Believe that you are right.
4. If you happen to be 220 yards from the green, and have decided that a mashie will do the job, make that decision definitive.
5. This method calls for mental training.

"Don't give another thought to any other club, or any change in power. Right or wrong, close your mind to any thought of change or the possibility of a mistake."

—*Grantland Rice*

On Practice

By Harold Hilton

I've always been a great believer in practice. In fact, I consider that the present position I hold in the golfing world is in a very great measure due to the faculty I am gifted with, of being able to proceed out to some quiet corner of the links, with just a couple of clubs and a dozen balls, and religiously set myself to the task of trying to find out the peculiarities and idiosyncrasies of these particular weapons. To many this procedure may seem a somewhat dull and uninteresting task, but personally I've always found it to be a most fascinating form of pastime. I must candidly acknowledge to enjoying even to this day an hour all alone by myself on the links more than the pleasure of participating in the most interesting and pleasant match one can imagine.

My attention was first called to the value of practice by British amateur, Mr. A. F. Macfie. As a small boy I remembered him as a player with a handicap of ten or 12 strokes. There seemed no great likelihood of his ever becoming a really first rate golfer. He was not a particularly young man and was a man of remarkably slight physique, but he overcame these natural obstacles by a grim determination to conquer the game at any cost. He won the inaugural amateur championship which was held at Hoylake in 1885, defeating in the final round Mr. Horace Hutchinson by 6 & 4. It was an extraordinary feat for a player who but a few years before was in receipt of a comparatively long handicap. He won by the extraordinary mechanical accuracy of his game. By assiduous thought and practice he made himself into a golfing machine.

His success was due to a determination to conquer the game, allied with the faculty of being able to spend hour after hour in solitary practice. One would see him out early in the morning and late at night, with two or three clubs and numberless balls, playing the same class of shot for hours on end.

Of course you have your repetition of Mr. Allan Macfie in the person of Walter Travis. I've been told that in the early days of his career he would pass hour after hour playing individual shots. Although he had a natural aptitude for the game, still his success was in a great measure due to constant practice.[50]

"A young player is apt to gain more knowledge practicing in solitude than he is likely to acquire in playing 36 holes against even the finest players in the world."
—*Harold Hilton*

---

50 Harold Hilton in "Practice in Golf, The Value of Consistent Training to Beginners and Others," *The Outing Magazine*, August 1912, p. 597.

The Golfer's Tale

During the 1915 US Open, Jerry Travers sliced his ball out of bounds at the 10th tee of Baltusrol. He was one stroke in front of the field. He hit his drive from an elevated tee toward a fairway leading to an island green some 300 yards away. According to Grantland Rice: "Travers was undecided whether to use a mid-iron to allow for a fuller pitch, or a driving-iron that would get more distance but would also leave a more delicate shot across the water. He finally decided to use a driving iron with only a three-quarter stroke, but he was still debating the matter as he swung the ball. Yet as he studied his lie in the rough and finally took his stance, it was easy to see that his concentration on the third shot was unbroken. Insofar as one could tell he had forgotten his two mistakes completely. The result was a pitch from the rough to within two feet of the pin and par 4 after two successive errors." Travers scored 37 in the back nine and won the championship with 297 strokes, just one stroke over par for 72 holes. (The par of Baltusrol was 74.)

"I believe I never played a short chip from just off the green that I did not feel that I would hole it in. It was not just hope but actual expectation."

—Jerry Travers

Practicing a
Controlled Slice

The flight of a golf ball is about geophysics. Light travels in a straight line. But it is the only thing that does. Golf balls don't. Golf balls are physical things that obey the laws of nature, like any other physical things. They follow the curvature of the earth. Eight hundred and thirty yards is a significant piece of curvature. The ball is by the club-head and rises above the line of sight, then it passes through it, then it falls below it, in a perfect curve, like the earth. Except it is not a perfect curve, because the very first millisecond the ball is hit, gravity is plucking at it like a small insistent hand. The ball can't ignore it. It is a 1.620-ounce three-piece, plastic-cover ball, traveling at nearly 200 miles an hour, but gravity has its way—not very successfully, at first, but its best ally soon chips in: Friction. From the very first millisecond of its travel, air friction is slowing down the ball and handing gravity a larger and larger say in its destiny. Friction and gravity work together to haul that ball down. That is why it is better to practice a little self-denial in driving, Walter Travis said, and keep the ball straight, so you don't try to avoid the effect of pull and slice. You master them. Gene Sarazen wrote down these reflections:

"It is one thing to be able to slice a golf ball and another to control the slice. The average beginner, failing to keep the elbows close to the body, is prone to cut across the ball, which invariably produces a slice. That isn't the kind of sliced shot I was after. What I set out to develop and what I needed was the kind of slice that had a slight fade-away to the right. I decided to change the position of the ball instead of the position of my feet. I moved the ball to and from until I had located the right spot, almost opposite the heel of my left foot. In other words, I found that by playing the ball more off the left foot than the right, and by cutting across the ball slightly, I got the results I desired. I play most of my shots with the ball almost opposite the center of my stance. Finding I could slice a ball playing in the manner described above, I practiced and practiced on the shot until I had it perfected."

How to "Correct" a Slice

Option 1: Hit to the right purposely. Swing the club-head along an inside-out line toward the right of the intended line of play.

Option 2: See that the hands are not ahead of the club-head, thus causing the club to draw across the ball.

Option 3: If at the moment of impact, the club is held equally tight with both hands there will be little likelihood of a pull or a slice.

Option 4: Don't turn your shoulders too soon or pull themselves up as you hit the ball. Both faults are born from the desire to hit.

Option 5: Throw the weight well forward on the left leg in taking the stance, and keep it there practically throughout the entire stroke (Jim Barnes very often used to give this advice).

Option 6: Concentrate upon holding the swing behind the line of flight passing through the ball (Bobby Jones).

Option 7: Hold the left side firm, not only to forbid the left hip to relax and fall away, but to compel it to point in the direction of the hole at the finish of the swing (Roger and Joyce Wethered).

"At the actual moment of hitting the ball, the eye performs an invaluable service by consciously focusing the mind on the ball and thus counteracting any inclination to hurry or get in front of the stroke."

—Joyce and Roger Wethered

A Lesson
with Harry Vardon

- In its upward movement the head of a club should take a line distinctly outside that which is taken in the case of an ordinary drive.
- The club takes the same line on the return, and after it has struck the ball, it comes inside the line taken in the case of the ordinary drive.
- At the moment of impact and for the fractional part of a second during which the ball may be supposed to be clinging to the face of the club, the face of the driver or brassie is being drawn across the ball, as if cutting a slice out of it.
- The time during which the slicing process is going on, is long enough to effect a great change in what happens afterwards.
- In that short space of time a spinning motion is put upon the ball which sooner or later takes effect.
- When a distance slice is wanted, the same principles of striking the ball and finishing the swing as govern the ordinary drive are to be observed.
- A distance slice is one in which the ball is not asked to go around a corner until the tree, or whatever it is that has to be negotiated, is halfway out or more.

This is the most difficult kind of slice, as the ball must be kept on a straight line until the object is approached and then made to curl round it as if it knew how.

The club should be drawn very gradually across, and not so much or so suddenly as when the slice is wanted immediately.

If the tree or other thing that stymies you is only 20 or 30 yards away, the short sliced shot is not only the best but perhaps the only one to play.

Properly done, the intentional pull and slice is a splendid thing to see and results in a real gain to the player.

FOR THE PULLED BALL
1. Move right around to the front of the ball.
2. Bring your right foot into a line with the ball. This foot may also be a little behind the left.
3. It helps to put the hands in front of the ball when the address is taken.
4. Hold the club more loosely with the left hand than with the right.
5. The head of the club should be carried just along the line in the upward swing.
6. At the moment of impact the right hand should begin to turn over smoothly and naturally; anything in the nature of a jab would certainly prove fatal.
7. At the finish the right hand has gained final command and is well above the left.[51]

"One of the surest ways of producing a slice is to aim the ball for the left of the course with the left foot well back and the shoulders lined up in a slanting direction."

—Jim Barnes

---

51 Vardon, Harry. "Harry Vardon on Pulling and Slicing," *The American Golfer*, July 1916, pp. 175, 176, & 177.

A Fairway Story

By Grantland Rice

Some time ago I watched Tommy Armour giving a golf lesson. After a few slight corrections in the pupil's stance and grip, there was one main idea he worked on, stroke after stroke: "Swing the club-head away from you; hit to the right." Armour had his pupil stand as if about to drive down the middle of the fairway. He then picked out a tall pine tree just at the edge of the course, to the right of the fairway. "Now," he said, "I want you to hit the ball in the direction of that pine." The pupil did as told, and much to his surprise the ball after starting slightly to the right, finished with a slight hook near the center of the fairway.

The Rhythmic Cycle of Coordination

Sir Ernest Holderness described four types of golfing temperament:

1. The sanguine (the phlegmatic being but with a degree of the sanguineous)
2. The melancholic (that include the choleric)
3. The nervous and the artistic temperaments are in the balance
4. The poetic

The poetic temperament is the worst, according to Sir Walter Simpson, for first "it dreams of brilliant drives, iron shots laid dead, and long putts held, whilst in real golf success waits for him who takes care of the foozle and leaves the fine shots to take care of themselves." What is the power by means of which the golfer exerts control over his game? Is it another sort of optimism? Simpson was committed to the thesis that it takes more than one poor shot to ruin a game or spoil a score. And he took it for granted that a poor shot at the tee might result in a lucky putt.

J. Sherlock was inclined to think that control was certainly an indispensable factor in the successful golfer:

"Control in a sense which I will endeavor to explain, and this, at any rate, it is within the power of most to develop; and yet how many practice it? To half the golfers, I would say, it is not practice with the club you need, but practice with the man; it is not skill you lack, but control. And out of control will grow confidence, which can hardly be described as a cause but an effect; and if there is one truism in this game of golf, it is that confidence is more than half-way to success."[52]

P. A. Vaile acknowledged:

"What is called 'the golf temperament' is not so much what is born in a man as what a man can school himself to be. It is merely another way of saying that one is a good-natured sportsman who cheerfully takes the rough luck with the good things that come his way. There is never anything on a golf links about which it is worthwhile to be seriously angry. I know that there will be some golfers who will question my logic, but this I believe all will admit that it is very stupid to lose control of one's temper, for the only result is that one helps the opposition."[53]

"There is a big difference between mere nervousness and a violent inward explosion of wrath or peevishness."

—Grantland Rice[54]

BURST OF ANGER: The ability of an athlete to put himself across in a big way when he is mad. For there is something about the emotion of getting mad that sends through the athlete's body

52 J. Sherlock in "Temperament and Other Matters That May, or May Not, Help One's Game," *Golf, USGA, Bulletin*, February 1917, pp. 85–89.

53 P. A. Vaile in "Can a Man Improve His Golf After Forty?" *Golf, USGA Bulletin*, February 1917, pp. 73–78.

54 Grantland Rice in "British Ways, and Ours," *The American Golfer*, August 27, 1921, p. 30.

all his surplus energies. Bobby Jones said, "Your game will never improve until you learn how to curse a little when shots go bad." His famous putter, Calamity Jane, not only had the loft of a 2-iron, but it also, as Harvey Penick has come to understand it, a lot of tape and glue on the shaft because Bob broke it several times.

Ten Common Faults in Golf

1. Failure to keep the head down and hold it still.
2. Failure to keep eyes on the ball.
3. Failure to carry club-head back straight and near the ground for at least first 12 inches of the backswing.
4. Failure to keep the arms straight.
5. Failure to hit square and to follow through.
6. Failure to "time" the shot properly.
7. Failure to take sufficient time, especially in the backswing.
8. Failure to keep all muscles lax, easy, and free.
9. Failure to keep the body balanced throughout the shot.
10. Failure to putt for the back of the cup.

"The older one gets, the greater the tendency to lift the club with the right hand."

—*MacDonald Smith*

QUICK CURES

Grantland Rice was convinced that it would be very much like editing a dictionary if one is going to totalize the entire list of golfing faults. Yet he summarized the following remedies:

1. If you are slicing, start the hands to work sooner on the downswing and keep the weight back on the right heel longer.
2. If you are hooking, address the ball in the heel of the club and think of hitting it in the heel.
3. Try a lighter finger grip and a smoother backswing.
4. Think of swinging through the ball, not where the ball is going.

MIND POWER: Visualize a trap, and that is where the ball goes.

Lack of Timing

- **Hitting too soon and putting the punch in too quickly:** This over-eagerness gets the body in ahead of the hands and kills the force of the blow.
- **Lack of timing:** Due to one of two things. The average player is either stiff or halting on his swing or else is fast and jerky.
- **Lack of team play between arms and body:** Lack of team play among the hands, arms, and body where one or the other either gets into the picture too quickly or else too slowly.

"There is a big tendency to hit too quickly. But if the backswing is properly timed and is smooth and even, the downswing is likely to be properly timed, too. Concentrate on getting the right backswing, on getting the left shoulder in place back of the ball and on getting more freedom into the stroke."

—Alex Smith

- One of the best ways to correct a fault is to learn how to make a fault. Indeed, it is only after you've learned how to play a slice or a hook that a cure for both will begin to emerge.
- Once you know how it is done the rest of it is fairly simple. Correcting a fault that is 90 percent mystery is an achievement that is rarely accomplished.

- If you have hit upon a satisfactory remedy do not attempt to improve upon it. The more often you play a shot, the greater the certainty that some error will appear.

Teaching Golf
Is to Learn Twice

Winning is a sweet, wonderful reward, but what of its price? Harry Vardon was 12 when he began to feel the pressure and responsibility to go out to work and thus do his bit toward the maintenance of the home. They were a big family of six boys and two girls. At that time, he did not have the slightest thought of taking golf seriously. The Royal Jersey Golf Club in Grouville opened in 1878, prompting most of the boys in the village to dabble in the game. His collection of clubs did not include irons and putters. He manufactured only some homemade clubs in which a stick from a blackthorn served as the shaft and a piece of oak as the head. They bored a hole in the head with a red-hot poker to insert the blackthorn stick and tightened the joint with the aid of wedges. He had no time for practice. He served as page-boy for a doctor at the age of 13 and performed several other duties (like helping to make butter) so that he did not play golf at all for the next four years. He said, "When I was 17, I went as gardener to Major Spofforth, a brother of F. R. Spofforth, the famous Australian cricketer, who was known as The Demon Bowler." Seeing Harry's passion for golf, Major Spofforth felt great admiration and took him to play. Major Spofforth gave him some of his old clubs and encouraged him not to give up golf, for "it may be useful to you some day," he said. Vardon entered a competition for a vase given by the local working men's club at 20. For six months, they had to play one round a month and he won easily. His most cherished trophy—because it was the first—was destroyed when a German airman dropped a bomb at the back door of his home at Totteridge.

Vardon recognized it was a very good thing for a young golfer to learn the swing at the time when the imitative faculty of the young mind is at its best. While he emphasized his passion and prowess as a teacher of the game and he expressed his willingness to mentor young golfers, he neither exaggerated the importance of growing up from babyhood "teethed on a golf club handle" nor of diligent, everyday play. He was not guilty of heresy nonetheless. He instructed others in the game, each one according to his skills. Vardon said:

"Children cannot be taught golf but they are born mimics and if you put them into good company, they will grow up in the right way. You must let them do as they will for a time—at any rate, on the links—and then, when they grow to the age of 14 or 15, you can give them hints that will make them advance rapidly. At home I studied the styles of the golfers I saw because it seemed natural to do so, but I cannot say that I molded my methods on those of anybody in particular. I never had a lesson and cannot recall anybody who impressed me as being a model who should be copied.

"There is some mystery about the consistency with which the Jersey golfers have adapted themselves to the upright swing—that compact manner of wielding the club which came as a shock to the people who for years had worshiped the longer and flatter method, known as the Saint Andrews swing. I never thought about the matter until I obtained my first professional post at Ripon, Yorkshire. And it was when I was 21 and in my second appointment at Bury, Lancashire, that I began to study and learn golf in real earnest."[55]

55 Harry Vardon in "Recollections of My Early Golf," *Golf Illustrated*, June 1922, pp. 16, 17, & 46.

1900

In 1900, Vardon made more money playing golf than any other person on the planet. Spalding engaged Vardon for a tour in United States. The matches began on February 12 in Perth Amboy, New Jersey, and ended December 10 in Colorado Springs, Colorado. He would play at new country clubs, in mountains and near seashores. Vardon lost at least 15 times over 80 or so matches. Opponents included three US Amateur champs and four of the first five US Open winners. His exhibition fee, arranged by Spalding, was $250. He outdistanced nearly every professional he played against. A 230-yard drive was breathtaking. Average drives of the day with the guttie were about 150 yards.[56]

"His words inspired my teachings and did a lot to help me win the US Open eight years after Harry Vardon gave me this tip: 'Take more club, grip it shorter, and hit within your power.'"

—*Johnny Farrell*

---

56 Primary source: Review by Jim Davis of *The Vardon Invasion*, by Bob Labbance with Brian Siplo, 2008, Sports Media Group: https://www.hickory-golfers.com/the-vardon-invasion_5177_ct.aspx

The Answer

By O. B. Keeler

It was in the second qualifying round of the 1920 United States Open Championships, the first in which Bobby (Jones) played. He was qualifying with Harry Vardon and they had tied the first round. He finished the round well, and led Vardon for the 36 holes, and that night at the hotel I went over to his table. I wanted to learn what the great Vardon had said about his playing. I knew all the folks at home would be expecting some comment on their kid wonder from the Old Master whom he had led in the qualifying round.

"Bobby," I said, "What did Vardon say about your game?" Bobby's ears got red again.

"Nothing," said he, positively.

"Come on, Bobby," I said. "Don't bother about being modest. Tell me just what Vardon said, and I'll fix it up so nobody who reads will know you told me. What did he say?"

"Do you want to know just exactly what he said?" returned Bobby.

"Just exactly," I assured him. "I'll look after your juvenile modesty for you."

"Well, I'll tell you. You remember that rotten topped approach shot across the seventh green?"

I did, without effort.

Well, as we were walking to the eighth tee, I said: "Mr. Vardon, did you ever see a worse shot than that?" And he said: "No." And that was everything he said about my game.[57]

SET THE MIND TO WATCH THE MIND: To have a feeling of perfect confidence in every shot, with a foreknowledge that what has been done well once can be well repeated. How we achieve this on the course is another question. Having pointed to the importance of relaxing the whole body, John Taylor concluded that a player must never allow the mind to wander from the job at hands: "He must play with the same concentration in the third as in the first day, or whether he be six up or six down."

---

57 O. B. Keeler in "A Tale of Two Champions, Harry Vardon & Bobby Jones," *The American Golfer*, May 2, 1925.

Dead Hands Is the Worst Fault in Golf

By Jack Rice

The golf stroke is a swing, not a hit. Touch must come through active hands and wrists. The main idea in golf is to have the hands swinging the club-head. Keep the body as relaxed as possible and let it follow the leader, which is the hands, throughout the swing. If your hands are working properly the body will work with them and not get in the way. Try to think more in terms of *live hands* rather than what the rest of the body might be doing.[58]

"You will find that the man who has a faulty grip is always trying to correct errors in his game. He never really gets to the root of his real fault—which is in his hands."

—*Gene Sarazen*

---

58 "The Worst Fault in Golf Is Dead Hands," *The American Golfer*, 1932.

Anxiety and Despair
at the US Open

Cyril Walker (1892–1948) was an English golfer born in Manchester. He came to the United States in 1914 and went on to become a promising young pro at the Englewood Golf Club in New Jersey. He won the US Open at Oakland Hills Country Club ten years later. This was his only top ten in seven appearances.

When the US Open began, Walker nearly experienced an early version of "choking" by the sporadic realization that this task may prove unattainable forever. He was not satisfied with his own game. "I lack . . . I don't know what," he said, and subsequently became absolutely frozen even thinking about playing an apparently simple chip. He took control of his nerves under the care of two physicians. On the final day, when the wind blew hardest, Walker played his best golf and beat defending champion Bobby Jones by three strokes.

He set himself into the right mental attitude. Whenever he stood on a green at Oakland Hills, Walker said to himself: "This one golf hole is the single problem of my career. It is the problem of my existence. There never has been any other problem. There never will be any other problem. I was created, developed, trained, drilled, to play this one hole in par. It shall be done."

That year, Walker and Hagen played a 72-holes-match at Saint Petersburg, Florida, for the unofficial crown of "champion of the world." Hagen was, then, the British Open Champion and defeated Walker 17 and 15. Of 57 holes played, Walker won 7 and tied 25.

Getting Out of Trouble

By Cyril Walker

It may be that in place of reaching a trap or a bunker you play into thick grass. Here are some suggestions to remember:

1. Be sure first that you are going to get well out, instead of taking any big risk with a straight-faced club.
2. If the ball is lying heavily where the grass is thick, try on the downswing to hit as close in back of the ball as possible. In other words don't hit too far back where the grass can form a cushion between your club-head and the ball.
3. Don't swing back too hurriedly, for this is another stroke that must be firmly played.
4. Don't ease up on the stroke. Let the club-head go through with a firm left wrist guiding the club.

Another important feature of this stroke is the mental attitude. If you believe you won't get out, you very likely won't. If you approach the test without any confidence or with a feeling of dread, you are not going to have very much luck.[59]

---

59 Cyril Walker in "Recovering from Difficulties—The Chip Shot," *The American Golfer*, June 4, 1921, pp. 15 & 26.

When You Least Expect

At the 1928 US Open, Johnny Farrell beat Bobby Jones by a stroke in a 36-hole playoff. Jones was the third-round leader by two, and Farrell was five strokes off the pace. But he shot 72 early, while Jones struggled to a 77. Farrell's recollection, which he told to Grantland Rice, editor of *The American Golfer*, was this:

"You can imagine my feelings when I heard that Hancock had two 5's to win. That was quite a shock. A moment before I was sitting on top of the world and now I was down in the depths of despair for I didn't see how anyone could possibly fail to get two 5's on the last two holes. Gene (Sarazen) and I strolled out toward the 16th green. I didn't know whether to watch Hancock or not for I didn't want to root against him and I certainly didn't want to root for him as you can readily understand.

"And when he took those two 6's I felt that fate was certainly playing into my hands and that my great opportunity had at last come. As a result of having played the first two rounds with Bobby I knew I was hitting the ball just as well as he was and I felt that I had a good chance.

"Then when I finished the morning round with a three-stroke lead on Bobby Jones as a result of having made four birdies in succession on the last four holes, I was even more confident when I started out on the final round; but not so confident when he caught me as a result of my taking three putts on each of the first two greens. As I walked over to the next tee I said to Tommy Kerrigan who had remained over for the purpose of giving me the benefit of his moral support: 'They all think I'm yellow. Well, I'll show them. I'm going to go to him now for I've got those putts out of my system.'"

There was a moment within the championship in which Farrell thought he was going to win. It was at the 14th hole of the last round where he hooked his tee shot badly and the ball went into the trees. But "just when my heart was about to sink down into my shoes" the ball dropped out into the fairway. "There's the championship," he said to himself. With two holes to go, Roland Hancock needed bogey-par to win. Instead Hancock went double bogey–bogey and finished in solo third, one stroke out of the playoff. Johnny continued:

"According to Tommy MacNamara, who was with me also, the second shot to the next hole (the 3rd) was the deciding shot of the play off. Anyway, it enabled me to get a 4 to Bobby's 6 and I had two of my three strokes back. I was still leading him two strokes when we turned as a result of his taking a 6 to my 4 on the 9th, which, by the way, was a bad hole for Jones throughout the tournament as was also the third. Then he squared me by getting a 4 on the 10th, and 11th to my 5. And he took the lead when I played my second shot too strong on the 12th and went over the green. I had always been short on this hole and I was determined to be up this time and hit the shot a trifle too hard.

"Things didn't look so good then and they looked worse when he pitched to within four yards of the pin on the 13th. I was in a tight situation now and I think the shot I played there was the shot that did the business.

"I also played the 15th perfectly. Bobby had a good break there for his drive looked to me to be headed for the ravine. When I saw the ball go I thought to myself 'it's all over now' and I received a great mental jolt when I heard someone yell: 'It's all right,' meaning that his ball had not gone into the ravine at all. It went through the trees, as I afterward learned, hit a spectator and dropped out almost in the fairway.

"He got a half with me there and then he dropped that stroke on the 16th, which left me one to the good with only two holes left. 'I'll hold him now,' I said to myself. And when I pitched out of the rough to within two feet (or so) on the 17th and came up on the green and saw his ball fully 30 feet from the hole and mine up there close I thought: 'Well, I'm in at last.'

"Imagine my surprise when Bobby said to the man holding the flag: 'Take it out' and then rammed down that long putt leaving me with that two-footer that now looked like at least a two-yard longer. I managed to get it down. And so we came to the last hole. I was in the rough on my drive and still in the rough, 50 yards from the green on my second while Jones was hole-high in two.

"A great deal has been written about the seven- or eight-foot putt that I holed after Jones had chipped to within a yard or so; a beautiful shot. But it was the shot before the putt that did the business. In other words it was the pitch to the green. For it was the pitch that left my ball in the best possible position, for I had nothing left but a straight up-hill putt. What did I think when the cameras started clicking as I took my stance? Why I just said to myself: 'You've got to make this one. Just loosen upon your grip and put it in.'

"And that's what I did. After that everything was a blank for a time and I didn't know much about what happened until I was being carried off the green on the shoulders of Sarazen, Kerrigan, Oscar Carlson, Bill Klein and Tommy Mac who had remained over for the play-off."[60]

---

60 Johnny Farrell in "You Win When You Least Expect To," *The American Golfer*, August 1928, pp. 8 & 57.

The Uncertainty of the US Open

By Bobby Jones

Golf is not the kind of sport or enterprise with which one would suspect that cruelty had any connection. Yet to the few who may be suffering through the last nine holes striving to finish before the strokes run out, the prospect of physical punishment would seem mild, indeed.

The ideal competitive temperament is difficult to describe or recognize. The intense strain imposed by the knowledge that a shot must be brought off or a much coveted prize lost, may affect different men in different ways. To one the strain is helpful because it keys him up. The importance of the thing overwhelms him and drives from his mind all thoughts save those concerned with hitting the ball and hitting it correctly.

The other poor fellow, strive though he may, cannot put from his thoughts what will happen if he fails, what he will lose, what he will feel. He cannot put away fear and anxiety long enough for concentration to have a chance. He cannot stop worrying about the result long enough to give attention to hitting the ball.

It would seem to be a simple matter to maintain a sufficient concentration throughout 18 holes today, another 18 tomorrow and 36 the next day. But it is difficult to appreciate how intense the effort must be, where the margin is often no more than a stroke or two in 72 holes.

The temptation to ease up, to give those tired faculties a rest, is sometimes overwhelming and always disastrous whenever it is yielded to. A wide expanse of airway confronted from the tee, or a simple three-foot putt down a groove have upset men who had conquered most difficult holes. The worst of it is that it is so easy to rest and yet one must not.

And as the average golfer follows the expert at the Open let him think a bit of his own troubles. They are exactly the same, only different in degree. Let him think how many strokes he could save by thinking of his left arm instead of worrying about the bunker at the right of the green, and by concentrating on striking his putt correctly instead of wondering what sort of a roll it would take. Let him overcome his anxiety to a point where he can give no more concern to result than is necessary to determine how he wants to hit the ball and then devote his entire attention to hitting it in that way.[61]

---

61 Bobby Jones in "The Pressure of The Open," *The American Golfer*, June 1932, pp. 11 & 53.

The Safer Stroke

By Grantland Rice

Bobby Jones, playing against (Bob) Cruickshank at the 17th hole at Inwood in the US Open playoff, found his tee shot in the edge of the rough, most directly behind a tree. He had three types of shots to play: 1) A pitch over the tree, a spectacular effort that might have yielded a 4 or a 6; 2) A hooked shot around the tree that might have found the green and might have led to deeper trouble; 3) A straight shot to the right corner of the green with a possible 4 and sure 5. Jones elected to play the safer shot. As it happened the ball bounded a trifle too far and found a trap. But he had at least worked upon the proposition of playing the easier stroke.

When we followed Vardon at Inverness on his east march where he played 28 consecutive holes in two under before the heavy wind came up, we found him playing each approach—not for the pin—but for the middle of the green. Many of the pins were placed near deep traps and Vardon was attempting no fancy and dangerous approaches under such conditions; he was also allowing greater margin of error.

What to Do
in the Face of . . .

- Inferiority complex
- Publicized stars who will make a better shot than you
- Missing shots and throwing away strokes
- A burst of applause from a distant part of the course
- The temptation to guess what someone else will do

Keep on hitting the ball, no matter what happens.

Looking at the leaderboard before the last round in the 1920 US Open at Inverness Club, Bobby Jones came to the conclusion that he must do a 69 at the most to have a chance; in reality, a 73 would have tied. He had a similar lesson every year until he finally decided that the best of them would make mistakes just as he did.

- The whole round is a competition against opponents who cannot be seen.
- Once a player sets off on a wild train of thought, he might as well give up.
- A player must get control of his mind and concentrate on the real job at hand.

"In an Open Championship one's imagination runs riot. A cheer from a distant part of the course is always interpreted as a blow from some close pursuer, when it may mean no more than that some obscure competitor had holed a chip shot while another player's waiting gallery happened to be watching. It may not mean a thing, and even if it does, it can't be helped."

—*Bobby Jones*

- In order to win the US Open, you must learn to putt on fast greens. And especially don't leave yourself long comeback putts.
- Play one stroke at a time.
- Think only of the next shot to be played—not on the missed shot or whether (or not) you have drawn bad luck to yourself.
- Self-doubt there may be, but it cannot always win the round.
- Everything in the US Open is improvisation.
- Creativity requires self-assurance and the ability to take risks.

"Rest the mind. Practice golf long enough to get on your stroke, and then relax. Lay off your game, dissipate mildly; play bridge."
—*O. B. Keeler*

Saving Strokes

- Don't try heroic measures except in desperate situations.
- Remember that the worse the lie, the more carefully and quietly should the stroke be played.
- Don't come to a lie on the rough blind with rage. That is a sure way to take a snappy six or seven and fade out of the tournament.
- Never use from the rough the same club you would use from the fairway.
- Make sure to get the ball back into play.

You must ignore your primordial instinct: Getting the ball up.

When a golfer is trapped, he is more than apt to dash into the trap with a spirit of revenge, and bristling with annoyance. He will generally emerge with two or three strokes added to his scorecard.

- Never take stupid risks. (You have lost a shot. Now, you might have lost three or four more by trying to get distance from the rough. Is that reasonable?)
- From a nasty lie, don't hesitate to use the sand wedge. (It will cut through virtually anything in the grass.)

- Don't put extra effort in the swing. (Give the club-head time to do its work, and do not dash it suddenly at the ball.)
- Be completely relaxed. Nothing must be cramped or stiff.
- When a shot goes wrong, the best thing to do is to retrieve the loss. Don't take dangerous chances.
- There is no point in risking total failure (by striking as hard as you can) if it is impossible to get into the green in one stroke.

"A golfer should blame himself for his misfortunes and give himself release from the very fancies of golf."

—Grantland Rice

Feel and Visualization

Golf is in many ways the most technical and sophisticated of the games. It elevates imagination and visual thinking from a secondary or supportive to a primary and central role. Visualization does not occur spontaneously, without preparation. It is made possible by a gradual process of learning. What matters is what kind of learning is involved. Horton Smith indicates that imagination in golf originates from your eyes:

- "You see the ball and the place where you want the shot to finish.
- Next, you make a mental note of the many variables that go into shot planning.
- Then you imagine the best route your ball should take to finish on target, and the flight pattern it should assume.
- Finally, you should imagine or sense how your swing should feel to produce this type of shot."[62]

The golfer is a visual thinker and whatever he makes with his clubs shall be visualized first, for he is at the pinnacle of his ability when his temperament enables him to make the most of his talent.

---

62 Horton Smith in *100 Classic Golf Tips* (2007) edited by Christopher Obetz for *Golf Digest* magazine, Rizzoli International Publications, New York, p. 222.

Get Out in One Stroke

By Harry Vardon

When the ground is very hard, it is sometimes a blessing in disguise to be in a bunker near the green. If you know your bunker, and are on good terms with your niblick, it is frequently better to be in the sand than on the grass. This remark is not mere philosophy. It is good advice. After a drought, it may be very difficult to make the ball stop on the green, even though you play a good approach from the fairway. If you know how to execute a bunker shot, you can take so much sand as to put an inevitable check on the ball and make it rise so sluggishly as to stop somewhere near the hole. For the average golfer, going into a bunker after he has taken six at a simple hole in a medal competition, will often ruin his card beyond all chance of redemption. He will try to do something wonderful in the hazard to avoid being debited with another six. The reward often comes as a shock: He gets a 7 instead of a 6.

The "Do or Die" Situation

By Walter Hagen

I have found that it is always possible to play one of three shots from any lie in the fairway, usually in traps and many times in the rough. I have divided these shots into three classes.

My N° 1 I called the "Do or Die," for it is the shot that must be dead to halve or win a hole in a tight match competition.

N° 2 is the "Average" shot. It is not designed to get dead, but cutting down the element of risk to an appreciable extent by eliminating much of the hazard that must accompany the "Do or die" effort.

N° 3 is the real "Safety first" shot and is worthy of any champion. In fact, if good golfers would spend more time experimenting with a wider range of shots, scoring in major events would be more consistent.

Let us assume that we find our ball in a trap guarding the green. The step side of the trap is between the ball and the flag. The green slopes down to the cup. If we elect to play the N° 1 shot (explode right for the pin) we have a chance of laying the shot dead, but we must also face an equal chance of not getting out of the trap. By playing a mashie-niblick, we have a chance to chip up onto the green, no dead but say 20 feet from the flag. This will assure us of a try for a long putt and this is what I call my N° 2 shot, for we have at least two chances of getting on the green to one chance of missing the shot.

We may half-top the shot, yet the force of the stroke will result in enough topspin to carry the ball up the sloping side of the trap and it will stop on the green. It is hard to completely miss this type of shot. It may be played too hard, causing the ball to roll clear across the green and trickle off into another trap, but chances are it won't. The odds are two-to-one in our favor—and 20-foot putts are made sometimes.

There is usually one extremely difficult "hump" or overhanging mound guarding each trap. The one we have elected to use in our shot classification has a tricky mound near the center of the highest part, and directly between the ball and the flag. We went over this mound with our N° 1 shot, veered slightly to one side, when we used our mashie-niblick for N° 2, but now we reach down in the bag and shake out our old "Safety First!"

When we tried N° 1, we realized the danger of not getting out, the necessity of imparting enough backspin to hold the ball, for you shall remember that the green slopes down from the ball to the cup. The knowledge of all that might go wrong with the shot does not help us in the ever-present battle with tension. We had more confidence when we selected our mashie-niblick and chipped around this forbidding hump, because the shot required less loft and we didn't have to worry about "cut." We also felt certain of getting within 20 feet of the flag.

Now we play old N° 3—"Safety First!" No possible chance of missing the shot, for we have examined the side of the trap and realize that very little over-spin will be necessary to make the ball climb the bank and stop on the green. The chances are it won't be close to the hole but we will be out of trouble and on the green.

For the average player, I recommend the N° 2 shot. It is much better to be within 20 feet of the cup than still in a trap, or off the green, thinking of a shot that went wrong and debating the chances of getting within inches of the flag on our next try. It will help on the next tee too! The same holds true off the green. Learn to use the right club to reach the green.

"Chances favor only the prepared mind."

—*Louis Pasteur*

Come Down
with All Your Power
Behind the Ball

There is something very peculiar at work in Saint Andrews. In describing how to recover from difficulties, Harry Vardon encountered a particular feature which could only occur in Saint Andrews: when the ground is hard at the infamous Road Hole (the 17th), the second shot should be played "at the foot of the slope in front of the green, run up, and hope for a 4, while feeling satisfied to take 5." But if the golfer feels he could adopt bold tactics, "it is better to go to the left in spite of the bunker that is there awaiting you than to play straight and submit yourself to the danger of finishing on the dreaded road."

Normally Vardon would have done such thing, for playing from the right of the green means in all probability a return to the bunker. Such probability does indeed exist. From the Open he drew a lesson:

"When Braid was in that bunker in the third round of the 1910 Open Championship, he took something like a bucketful of sand in order to play a shot of a few yards. People who were present declare that the very green trembled when his club crashed into the hazard." Braid gained a brilliant victory.

Born Golfer

At the age of five his style was developed, controlled, and compact. At ten, he was recognized as a gifted young golfer. He began to play in pro tournaments of more and more significance. At the age of 14 he looked like a master. He drove to kill the ball but he would play safe when it was necessary. He trusted his own instincts and was usually right. At the age of 17 he won the Open Championship. The second of four children, Young Tom Morris was born in Saint Andrews in 1851. His career reached momentum when he conquered "the Belt" by scoring three successive victories in 1868, '69, and '70. The Open, then, lapsed for a year. Resumed in 1872, Tommy won it for a fourth successive time, a feat never since matched. His was the first name engraved on the new prize, the Claret Jug, commissioned at a cost of £30 and still awarded to the winner today. He died on Christmas Day, 1875. The available evidence suggests that he died from some cardiovascular disaster, probably a ruptured aneurysm of one of the main arteries at the back of his chest. He was 24 years old.

The Way Champions Are

By O. B. Keeler

In some cases of perfect shots brought off under exceptional stress, the golfer is controlled by a mind that is not his usual golfing mind. When the stress is severe enough it puts the objective mind, with its tendency to fault, on one side and leaves the player not consciously thinking, while the subjective mind, which does not make mistakes, assumes command. I say it is just possible but only with very great golfers, of the stuff of which champions are made. It is just possible that that is the difference between champions and others.

Kidding Yourself

By Walter Hagen

Each golfer loses hundreds of strokes in a season by trying to save the situation with a miraculous shot. Miraculous shots rarely come off, especially from the average player who is never too sure of how to play a simple pitch. I've seen golfers who were not very good at a simple mashie-pitch or even a chip shot trying to play strokes that the best of us could not get away with. That is what I call Kidding Yourself. If you always choose to play against your human nature, you will be kidding yourself into trying something you know should never be tried. Perhaps I am too cautious. But I have already had some experience.[63]

When you choose not only the hardest shot but actually an impossible shot you are yielding to a mental strabismus that spoils all your subsequent play. Play always the surest shot to get out of trouble at the least cost.

63 "Courage Counts in Golf," *Golfers Magazine*, April 1928.

The Moral Effect

By Roger Wethered

The situation faced by one who thought that two putts could not fail to win the hole is more complicated when an opponent got his ball stone dead from a hazard near the green, where it was fondly imagined to be well out of the hunt, may have a direct and severely temperamental effect on a close match. In a flash, the match has been completely and dramatically reversed. Plans that had been confidently laid, have to be readjusted with starling suddenness on the discovery that, after all, two putts (and good putts at that), are desperately needed to halve it in the end.

- Never be afraid of a bad shot.
- Remember that very often, Harry Vardon played deliberately into a bunker in order to have the chance of laying the next shot dead.
- There is something to be gained by considering whether the trouble can be used to advantage.
- Consequently, allow yourself four or five poor shots in a round, though it is a cardinal sin to hit two bad shots in a row.

The Golfer's Tale

By Francis Ouimet

[Walter] Hagen may make a mistake on a hole but though this may cost him a stroke he sees to it that it will not cost more. One time Jesse Sweetser and myself had the pleasure of playing against Walter and Sarazen at Saint Albans Country Club, Long Island. Aside from the match itself the four of us were engaged in a medal competition. Playing the eighth hole Walter's second shot—played a bit too boldly—scampered across the green into a trap and nestled against the bank of the trap. It was a most awkward position to be in because he could not play his shot without at first hitting the bank of the trap.

After much care he played and the ball did not come out. Sweetser, Sarazen, and myself were nicely on in two and with Hagen still in the trap after playing three it looked as though we would pick up two strokes on him. That is just what did not happen. With a rare chip out of the sand he laid his ball up six or seven feet from the hole and got the putt. We did gain a stroke on him, but that was all. He saw to it that no more shots were wasted and this is what I mean by saving strokes. He could well have taken a 6 on that hole but didn't.

"The secret of Hagen's success has been due principally to the fact that he is a great stroke saver."

—Francis Ouimet

149

The Good Wife

By Francis Ouimet

Let a man be seized with an idea and he either conquers the world or makes of himself a most asinine fool. The hardest sort of knocks rarely convinces him of his error. But let him witness the bizarre experiences of a friend laboring under the delusions of a like idea, or something akin to it, and his awakening is both sudden and rude. At least, I found this so when I tried to teach my wife to play golf. No matter how difficult the task became I could not for the life of me come to a realization of the truth. But when two friends of ours, another married couple, jokingly arranged a mixed foursome battle between the two families on a certain day, I came face to face with the facts.

For the first time in two years I saw myself, through the other man as others might well have seen me in my effort to implant a love for the game in my life's partner. We had no sooner started this match than the doting young husband, keen to defeat his neighbors, could not resist giving advice to his mate. It was her play, a short mashie to the green which was trapped to the right. "Pitch to the left," he said to her, "so you will be sure to avoid that trap." There was nothing if not sound sense in his remark. But when his better half not only pitched to the left but sent the ball clear out of bounds in that particular direction, he made the fatal mistake of leaving himself open for censure by remarking, "Why did you do that?"

There was no loss of time in the reply that came to him. "Well, didn't you just get through telling me to play that way?" It was not many holes after that before another loving couple was not on speaking terms, and I can vouch for the fine character and broad-mindedness of either of them.

The very next day I hunted up the professional at our club: "Harry," I said, "for the past two years I've been secretly depraving you of part of your just dues, fees that you rightfully deserve in the practice of your profession, and all because I was silly enough to believe that I could not only teach my wife to play golf but interest her to a very great extent in the game. I would not confess this fact to you had I been successful. So I am going to turn the whole job over to you and give you a free rein."

This solved my problem as the idea proved a good one. Harry molded Mrs. Ouimet into a very fair golfer, one whom Harry claims never so much as disputed a point or a suggestion he offered to her. Now all this convinced me that it is next to impossible for a husband to teach his wife to play golf, or even to try to, for when the pupil knows the instructor so well there are apt to be perplexed situations arise which upset the even tenor of things.

Yes, I've been through the whole thing and I can highly recommend every husband following my advice in the matter of solving his Sunday golf problem just as I finally solved it. Though it would be foolhardy of him to begin as I began; I gave it to the club professional. If you once get your wife to consent to that all is well, for Harry tells me once they start they are just like men; you can't ever stop them.

"Golf," he says, "is an incurable disease once you try to hit the first ball." I know that proved the case in our family for when Sunday afternoon comes around in spring, summer or fall, there is no more talks of tea dates or anything like that. It is a case of golf that's what it is, and there is really nothing to worry about. All of which, Mr. Bridegroom is a tip worth to follow.[64]

64 Francis Ouimet in "Teaching My Wife to Play Golf," *The American Golfer*, October 22, 1921, pp. 3, 26, 27, & 28.

The Rules
of Match Play

- Every hole must be played as a match in itself.
- Disregard what you may have done previously.
- Often matches have been won by doggedly hanging on.
- Try to be calm and collected. Make up your mind that nothing, no matter how irritating, will upset you.
- Never worry or hurry when difficulties arise. Take enough time but don't be unnecessarily slow.
- Don't try experimental shots or a new system when your opponent is dormie.
- No interference from outside must distract your attention. A Champion needs terrific power of concentration. He must keep his mind completely on the shot to be made.

"The match that is carelessly played had better not be played at all."

—Henry Leach

- Try to play every shot through the green to the place that suits your game.
- You should never lose confidence on account of failure, but rather endeavor to diagnose, and find the causes with a view of increasing your knowledge. Nothing is more unsettling in

152

match play than your opponent's ability to hole-in putts from yards off.

- Give yourself a quick shake mentally and release the physical tension. There is a remarkable class of players who win matches which they apparently should lose.
- In playing through the green, avoid as far as possible getting in your opponent's line of sight when he is making his stroke.

Play to win the hole.

"I've always gone whole hog or nothing. I like to win."
—*Walter Hagen*

- A match gives you freedom. It's not the kind of freedom that comes from improvisation and being aggressive. It's a cumulative freedom. It is power for golfers who have persistence and faith.
- Remember that more matches are lost by carelessness at the beginning than by any other cause. Take more risks when you are down to your opponent than when you are up on him.
- If you win the first hole, try to forget all about it when you go to the second tee.
- Whether you are one up or one down should never enter into it at all, not even when you are dormie.
- Basic rule of thumb in the green: When both balls are near the hole but still not dead, do not propose your opponent to half the hole. You thus could lose the nerve and the ability for holing short putts.

Never give up.

The Art of Winning a Match

By James Braid

The Secret of Match Play: It is simply to play your steadiest and best, and not to care about the opponent's game until it is absolutely necessary to do so. Anyone who has not got a perfect golfing temperament to abide by will find this simple rule very difficult to follow.

Rules of Common Sense: One can hardly teach a man to be either a good match or medal player. The only thing one can do is to remind him of the applications of various rules that may be called common sense.

Don't Press Beyond Your Capabilities: Remember that you do not so often win holes as the result of your brilliant play as by mistakes that the other man makes. In the absence of a lucky break in your favor, do not play desperately in order to make a chance for yourself.

Play Short Or Go For It. Your Choice: Keep a very sharp eye on what your opponent is doing, and in a large measure your own play must be regulated according to his. The last chance for winning or halving the hole is in the short game. Only play short when it would be risking too much to go for all that there is.

NEVER UP, NEVER IN: This is a safe rule for the putting in every match. Why? Because a vast number of holes are lost when the player has two putts and thinks he can afford to be almost anywhere with the first one. The result is being short with the first putt, which causes you to fear missing the next one.

Covet Every Hole: Play for all you are worth at the start, and establish a lead. Even when you have got it and are nearing home, never for a moment slacken in the idea that you can afford to take it easily.

James Braid then offered the second set of priceless permanent rules of unwritten behavior during the course of a match:

- The very talkative golfer is more often a nuisance than not.
- The time between shots is better occupied in thinking out the problems of the next shot, rather than engaging in general conversation.
- When the match is delayed in the middle, the eyes should be given as much rest as possible.
- Don't occupy this interval by staring hard at the green in the distance, waiting for the couple ahead to hole out and get along.
- The best thing to do is neither to look ahead all the time nor at one's ball, but just to turn your back on the latter and look about.[65]

---

65 James Braid in "The Wisdom of Braid," *The American Golfer*, August 1916, pp. 269, 270, 271, & 272.

Theories of Match Play

By Harold Hilton

I have noticed that the majority of good match players are inclined to be very silent men, and in consequence it is safe to assume that the lack of conversation is a virtue in the playing of the game of golf, and the class of conversation which should be particularly avoided is that species of running conversations with friends and acquaintances who happen to be among the spectators. Learn to bear your ill fortune without appealing for sympathy, as sympathy extended to a man during the course of play is more apt to upset him temperamentally than to strengthen his purpose in any way. The most reliable of golfers always prove to be those who play the game from beginning to the end of it without allowing any outside influence to affect them in any way whatsoever. To some golfers it is a difficult procedure to follow out, but it is truly wonderful how a young player can strengthen his temperament by continuous schooling.[66]

---

66 Harold Hilton, quoted by Robert A. Birman in his review of *Modern Golf*, by Harold Hilton (1913), Northwest Hickory Players website: http://nwhickoryplayers.org/2015/02/harold-hilton-modern-golf-1913/

"Confidence is a great helper in golf. Let a player lose it and he is marked for slaughter. On the other hand, an attack of over-confidence is apt to be fully as disastrous. Overconfidence and carelessness are teammates."

—*Jerry Travers*[67]

---

67 Quoted in *Golf Magazine* online, "The Ten Commandments of Match Play," http://www.golf.com/instruction/10-commandments-match-play

How to Drive Your Opponent Out of His Game

By O. B. Keeler

I remember an old trick of the Haig. I saw it last, I think, at Pelham in the PGA Championship of 1923. The drives at what then was the third hole—a long one—were good and about even, except that Walter had a yard or two in range, so his opponent had to play the odd. Walter walked over to the ball with his caddy, looked carefully at the distant green, and picked out his big iron. His adversary saw it. Obviously, he reflected that if Walter could get home with a big iron, so could he. He tried it—and was worse than 30 yards short. Walter put up the iron, banged the ball with a brassie, and was well on.

The Patriarch of American Golf: George Wright

George Wright, who might well be called the "Father of American Sports" (for he made valuable contributions in baseball, tennis, ice hockey, and golf), became the first man in the United States to knock a ball around a field with a golf club in 1863 when he was a member of the Saint George's Cricket Club, the oldest in New York. Wright said, "There was a Scotsman who was a member of the team and often talked about golf. He had some clubs and golf balls and one day he and I went out beyond the cricket grounds with them, on a level field. It was a strange, new thing for me and I didn't know how to hold the clubs or hit the ball. But the Scotsman showed me how it was done and then gave me a club and walked over to the other side of the field. He hit the ball over to my side and I drove it back."

The More I Relax, The Luckier I Am

By Gene Sarazen

Keep your distractions to a minimum and make your business to look at every match not as something separate and apart but as a stepping-stone to the eventual scaling to the heights. One secret of match play greatness is to remain serene and unworried in the face of an unexpected rally, to continue playing golf regardless of situation or circumstance, from the first drive to the closing putt.[68]

---

68 Gene Sarazen in "The Door to the Cup," *The American Golfer*, January 1925, pp. 30 & 39.

An Opponent Surprised Is Half Beaten

By Stewart Maiden

The idea in match play is to get a man down, and then get him farther down. When you are one up try to be two up on the next hole; when you have him nine down try to get him ten down. Play to win every hole, right up to the stage when you may be compelled to play for a half, and then try to stick one up there for a single putt. Play for your best shot, not your safest.

- A good straight driver sometimes has the effect of making your opponent feel an inferior player. This is an extremely unsatisfactory state of mind.
- The holding of a good putt gives a feeling of greater confidence with the following stroke, particularly on the next tee, but also through the green and in the short game.
- The man who plays his approach first can probably settle the issue by making a good shot.
- The approach in the first two or three holes is of great importance.
- If the putts on the first two greens are comparatively short ones there is a good chance that the player will have acquired a better touch when called upon to make longer putts on subsequent greens.

- Every time a hole is unexpectedly won, lost, or halved the incident may be said to be a turning point.

MATCH PLAY PROVERB
7 up & 27 to play never won a match.

Q & A

Focusing on the Flag

Q. Which was the best round Harry Vardon ever played?
A. He had no hesitation in selecting as his favorite recollection the final of an open professional tournament at Newcastle, County Down, in Ireland around 1900. His opponent was John Taylor. Both were at the top of their games in those days. Vardon said:

"In the final round I felt that nothing could stop me. Taylor went out in 39, which was the par score for the first nine holes. He said afterward that he did not make a mistake, which was true. Newcastle was a long course in the era of the gutta-percha ball, which was then in vogue; and with its big sand hills, its many bunkers large and bold, and its narrow fairways with punishing bents on either side, it tempered its justice with very little mercy. I reached the turn in 32, and my pleasantest phase of the recollection is that the 32 seemed to be easy. Turning seven holes up, I won the match of 36 holes by 11 & 10.

"What was the moral of that happy day? Well, I know that, in those times, whenever I was within reach of the green with any club—brassie, cleek, or anything else—I saw only the flag and thought only of the flag. Having weighed up the situation, I simply focused my attention on the flag and then on the ball, and forgot everything else. I could put the ball within a yard or two of any place that I wished. And so the game was especially easy for me."

Q. What was the key element that made Vardon one of the real immortals of golf?
A. The overlapping grip. Gene Sarazen said, "Prior to Vardon's time, the players all used the old Saint Andrews's, or regular two-handed baseball grip. Vardon's theory was that the hands must work as a unit. With the old Saint Andrews's grip, you couldn't possibly swing your hands. In fact, you couldn't even say that the hands worked together. Such an act was impossible."

Q. According to Vivian Doran, what is the most important factor in the attainment of distance from the tee?
A. The rate of acceleration of the velocity of the club-head during the impact and not merely the quantity of force employed. Vivian could not conceive how this could be done except by holding some force in reserve for release as nearly as possible at the moment of impact. She said, "The problem of long driving then is that of increasing the quantity of force employed while at the same time maintaining the rhythm of the stroke, that is, distributing the additional force in the proper ratio."

Q. Which is the governing feature of the slicing shot as the stance and the position of the golfer are concerned?
A. According to Vardon, the player must stand very much more behind the ball than when making an ordinary straight drive or approach, being the general effect of this stance to move the body slightly around to the right. He said, "There is no mystery as to how the slice is made, it comes simply as the result of the face of the club being drawn across the ball at the time of impact, and it is just in this way that it is done when it is not wanted."

Q. According to British golfer Cecil Leitch, what is a common fault among women and one that causes "socketing," "digging," and even "topping"?
A. To hit the ball entirely with the wrists and not letting the club-head do its work. Cecil, a self-taught golfer who shares a record with Joyce Wethered for winning four British Ladies Amateurs

titles, wrote: "There may be some excuse for a cricketer contracting this bad habit, but he or she who does not play cricket must remember when attempting to play golf that the club-head is the part with which the ball must be hit. Nearly every lady golfer is inclined to 'press' and 'dig' in order to raise the ball during the winter months. I would argue that a golfer is not really a golfer unless or until he grumbles without a cause. A smooth swing is all that is wanted to send the ball upon its way, and she who finds herself digging at the ball should look for the fault in her own swing and not blame the course." Cecil Leitch preferred to play in the wind. To be more precise, she changed the way women played golf in the 1920s by hitting hard (as opposed to daintily), which was a turning point in their game.

What to Do if You Are Off Your Game

By Walter Hagen

Going to a championship or any other tournament I may be on my game, or not so much on it, or positively off it. Golfers know what that means, you either are, or you are not. You cannot help it; physical condition means comparatively little in regulating it. And nobody is on all the time. Well, then, I go to a tournament, and I'm off. What to do? They won't postpone the tournament to wait for me to get my game. I've got to play. In the first round I'm not trying for anything beyond what I know is well inside whatever game I have at the time. If I am not driving well, I try to keep the ball well in the fairway. If I am not pitching well, I don't aim for the pin; instead I try for the green. If I am not putting well and the touch is lacking, I don't try to get the long ones down. Only to get them close enough to be sure of the next one.

How to Make the Game Harder

By Grantland Rice

1. Brooding too long over any mistake.
2. Failing to accept bad luck as a part of the game.
3. Eliminating yourself in advance on some hole when your ball reaches the rough or a deep trap.
4. Trying to hit too hard against the wind, thereby putting your body ahead of the stroke.
5. Hitting your shots before you've decided definitely just how hard you want to hit it.
6. Being over-anxious and therefore hitting too soon, applying your power in advance of the proper place.
7. Permitting a sudden upset on some hole to throw you off balance and produce a panicky state of mind.

"I can't emphasize this too strongly; the important point is learning your own game and not some other player's."

—Alex Smith[69]

---

[69] Quoted by H. B. Martin in *Vanity Fair*, January 1918, p. 57.

Q & A

Cheating the Wind[70]

Q. Are modern golfers familiar with how, in the beginning of the 20th century, the wind-cheater stroke was considered the master stroke in golf?

A. While it has been given an unimportant position in every book on golf instruction, the master stroke in golf that stands out above and beyond all others in its demand for accuracy and a perfect method of applying spins, it is the stroke which is commonly called a "wind-cheater." This is a stroke that excites and baffles the golfer's imagination, for it will require a supreme ability and perfection in the application of spin. The ball will fly very low, very close to the ground for the greater portion of its journey and then will rise toward the end of its flight to its greatest height. Vaile said, "Although this ball is called the wind-cheater, it is just as effective and just as useful on a perfectly still day as it is against a howling gale, for this stroke is, in my opinion, without any doubt whatever, the master stroke in golf. This stroke will make pull and slice practically unnecessary if a man has full command of the plain drive without back-spin and the wind-cheater. As the club is not at the lowest portion of the swing when it struck the ball, the wind-cheater acquires a large amount

---

70 "Along the Fairways," *The Lewiston Daily Sun*, April 12, 1928.

of back-spin, causing the ball to reach the highest point in its trajectory towards the end of its flight."

Q. What is the surest way for a golfer to be undone by his own industry?
A. Bobby Jones said, "The surest way to disturb the smoothly working mechanism is to interpose conscious control. In the case of nine people out of ten, I believe that trying to discover what is producing the good results would put them entirely off. The man would say to himself, 'How I am doing this?' and 'how am I doing that?' until he would be undone by his own industry; quite evidently he has been swinging correctly and just as surely will he continue to swing correctly if he will let himself alone. His muscles have formed a healthy habit which they will not give up unless interfered with."

Q. Why is imagination considered to be a handicap for a golfer?
A. It has been considered a handicap because of the necessity for subconscious control of the swing. Bobby Jones said, "The man with an obstructive imagination cannot help seeing the dangers and disasters which await him if he strays from the path. To that extent he is intent upon avoiding them and his concentration is destroyed. And this concentration which is so necessary is not concentration upon the swing but upon the results of the swing. It must be so complete that there can be no thought of technique."

Q. Why should young players avoid imitation in golf?
A. Because to be successful in golf, and though the technique for playing, say, an iron-shot to the green are the same, you must first know just what you can and cannot do with each club in your bag. Wrote Francis Ouimet, "I am not quite sure that my good friend Jerry Travers would never have been such a wonderful golfer had he attempted to imitate the play of many of his opponents during the big matches he so frequently won. Time and again Jerry would face players who obtained distances from the tee with the wood but when Jerry could not get his wood going

well, he never fell into the trap of trying to match them stroke for stroke, even though their drives were splendid ones. Jerry would play the game as he knew he could play it. He simply knew what he could do with each club in his bag. He was never concerned with what other stars could do with such and such a club. That was the dominating factor in his success, just as it is the dominating factor in the ranking of any fine golfer."

Q. Why could you benefit your game by demonstrating the scissors action of the hands and wrists during the golf stroke with an umbrella?

A. You will readily see how the club-head is given its speed as its goes through the ball. Wrote Chester Horton: "If you swing an umbrella with both hands traveling together the action of the tip of the umbrella will be the same as at the part you hold in your hands. But if you push the left hand back while the right hand is pressing forward, the far end of the umbrella will immediately assume great speed of action. In the golf stroke you should have a sense of trying to 'arrest' the movement of the left arm at the ball on the downswing. At the point is where the right side exerts the maximum of pressure on the club shaft and sends the club-head crashing through the ball. The left arm continues to go forward to the ball, but in reality it travels against resistance and the greater this resistance the harder the ball will hit. It resists the pressure of the right side of your body. You will attain the maximum of speed with the club-head if the end of the shaft held by the left hand could actually be anchored while the right side of your body is pressed forward." (Warning: do not demonstrate scissors action with an open umbrella.)

Q. Does looking up produce a bad swing or does a bad swing make you look up too soon?

A. Grantland Rice said, "The majority of the mistakes in golf are made well before the club-head ever gets to the ball. When the head is lifted too soon, as a rule it starts up before the club-head is within six inches of the ball, thereby throwing the swing out of line and killing most of the power of the punch. The common fault of hitting too soon usually begins with a backswing that is too fast or too jerky and this destroys any chance for rhythm later on. Or it may lead to the mistake of applying power too quickly on the downswing where all acceleration is choked off before the club-head ever gets the chance to speed up on its way through and beyond the ball."

Q. How much credit is Stewart Maiden due regarding the development of Bobby Jones's game?
A. It is difficult to deny that Maiden was a trainer of golf champions. He taught Jones and Alexa Stirling how to play different clubs. He showed them the swing, and, as Innis Brown wrote, "warned them against troubles that were likely to arise, and gave them the remedies for correcting such troubles. Then Maiden turned them loose to work out their own progress." Would it not be wiser to believe that Maiden followed the most logical and common-sense method of bringing them along, when indeed he took both when they were very young had them no natural faults and few (if any) physical limitations? Maiden, therefore, did not teach a method but allowed them to work out their own techniques of applying the underlying principles in the mechanical end of the game.

Q. What was the ball's behavior when Walter Hagen hit his tee-shot on one of the holes at Deal during his first Open Championship in 1920?
A. The ball stayed up in the wind so long that he turned his back on it to keep from being smacked in the face when the wind carried it back toward him: "At Deal I had played shots where the wind picked the ball up and almost slapped it back in my face. I needed a catcher's mask; that shot did not even carry to the rough in front of the tee."[71] The whipping, blustering wind was a new and puzzling experience for him.

---

71 Walter Hagen in *The Walter Hagen Story, By The Haig Himself as Told to Margaret Seaton Heck* (1956), Simon & Schuster, New York, p. 80.

Q. Why did Joyce Wethered feel annoyed on those occasions when she asked her brother Roger how the game ought to be learned?
A. Joyce said: "Because his invariable answer was that it was no use telling me anything, since I should never be any good until I found out things for myself. The principle he expressed was sound. For the golfer who asks, 'What am I doing wrong?' is expecting an answer which will supply a cut-and-dried remedy, some specific which will immediately effect an infallible cure. This can be rarely done. Golf is an art and a matter that closely concerns the individual. So it is necessary for everyone to discover the nature of their own faults."

"In true driving, the right arm has to accommodate itself in the swing back. It is loose and obedient. When the club is brought back to within a foot of the ball, the right arm joins with the other in the work of driving. After impact the right arm becomes master, the other slave."

—Sir Walter Simpson[72]

---

[72] Sir Walter Simpson in "Driving," *The American Golfer*, July 1918, pp. 776–779.

Cracking the Ball a Mile

"I have made many shots of gratifying length."

—Harry Vardon

- The long ball depends primarily on the speed of the club-head when it connects with the ball. It should strike the ball exactly in the center as though fired from a gun.
- Long driving makes putting easier.
- For a short driver the second shot will be much more difficult. Two extra putts, at least, will be taken from an average distance of forty feet.

"In the course of a round a player, whose second shot brought him to say an average of 25 feet from the hole, would quite likely average two's for the round of putting green strokes."

—John Anderson

- Golfers don't look for great distance because of their desire to hit the ball hard but because of the results of great desire.
- Nothing thrills you more than to be driving sweet and clean from the tee. This is what makes a drive shot unlike any other.

Drive's Equation:

Control + Balance = Timing

Hit Hard

- Don't make the mistake of getting out of your ordinary swing when you attempt to hit the ball hard. The body will sway ahead of the club-head on its way to meet the ball.
- Transmit your weight into club-head speed only.
- The club-head is what connects with the ball and you must work up velocity and not force.
- Put in your tee-shot as much power as you can control.
- Very often you will make the surprising discovery that you will gain more distance with less effort. It is proof that the stroke was correctly timed.
- Centralizing the power of the stroke immediately when the ball is reached and carrying it through the ball could increase distance.
- Do not ease up on the swing.
- Keep up the steam until the arms are well away on their upward journey.
- To me, says Walter Travis in effect, the follow-through plays a very important part in the length of the drive as well as in straightness.

"When they address the ball on the first tee, a large percentage of golfers who score over 85 habitually have a common thought: 'Hand me a driver and let me give the ball a ride.'"

—*Bobby Jones*

According to Walter Travis, the secret of long driving is in the easiness and velocity with which the weight of the body and arms is transferred from the left leg to the right and back again, joined with wrist action. He rather favored driving off the left leg because it was easier to get the arms and body around in the upward swing without the hitch that is produced "about three-quarters of the way up when the right foot is in front."

Vivian Doran found that the more keenly she pursued the ideal of hitting a ball high into the wind, the shorter it will travel. Golfers will get better results on low drives than by hitting high into the air. She said, "We will consider the case of a ball hit to carry 200 yards, the distance would be traversed in five seconds, and a simple calculation will show that the average speed of the ball must have been approximately 82 miles an hour— much greater, of course, for the major portion of the journey and slowing down a bit toward the end. The ball would be helped, of course, but the assistance would consist of a lessening of the normal atmospheric resistance to be overcome and this assistance would be present in the case of a low-hit ball, since there can be no very great difference in wind velocity at heights of, say, 20 and 50 feet."

Look for the Cause

By George Duncan

When a player is driving badly, it is quite likely that he is taking his eye off the ball. But it does him no good to tell him so, or make him try hard to look at the ball. I don't believe in worrying about that. The thing to do is to search for the antecedent cause. One may be sure that he is doing something wrong in the earlier part of his swing that makes it almost inevitable that his eye should come off. Find out this something and get rid of it. When a man says to me in explanation of a bad shot, "I took my eye off," I say to him, "But didn't you do something at the very beginning of your swing that made you do it?" If only one can get to the top of the swing properly the eye won't come off. I can never remember having taken my eye off unless there was something wrong on the way to the top.[73]

"Most golfers are inclined to dance too much on the tee. Keep your feet still and you will play your shots better. I would advise wearing a heavy pair of shoes to correct this fault."

—*James Fraser*[74]

---

73 George Duncan in "How I Cure Faults," *The American Golfer*, January 14, 1920, pp. 6, 28, & 29. The article was an extract from *Present Day Golf* by George Duncan and Bernard Darwin, printed by courtesy of George H. Doran Company.

74 *Vanity Fair*, January 1918, p. 57.

Knock the Hell Out of It!

By O. B. Keeler

I've often heard Stewart Maiden, and once in a while Alex Smith, compress an hour's instruction into one common and forceful admonition, which, however, is by no means without its appeal to the mental side of the situation: "Knock the Hell Out of It!" This simple and direct admonishment may appear at first blush to be more of an abjuration than an appeal to the higher intelligence. But did you ever loosen up, and stand to the ball, and try it? I mean, really try it? The result might astonish you, I can vouch for this, though it is largely a vicarious experience, every golfer with great range and accurate direction in his big shots does that very thing.[75]

A LESSON FROM 1895—By James Dwight
"Don't try to hit very hard. The ideal drive is not a blow to the ball but a long, even, rapid swing. Bring the club back quietly without hurry, keeping the arms out from the body. If there is hurry in starting the downswing the result will be a jerk. If the club goes through its full swing after hitting the ball, you will be surprised to see how long a drive you can make. The longer the club's head

---

75 O. B. Keeler in "Hit It at Something!" *The American Golfer*, March 11, 1922, pp. 15, 30, & 31.

swings truly in the line that the ball is to go the more the chance that it will hit the ball right."[76]

76 Dwight, James (1895) *Golf: A Handbook for Beginners*, Overman Wheel Company, New York.

Be Sure to Smell the Flowers

Asked what he thought was the main cause of a golfer invariably winning his matches, Harold Hilton answered, "the gift of extreme concentration in the playing of every shot." Golf historians have been confident about the matches to be gained by the power of concentration, believing it was somehow a natural gift, one of those instinctive abilities which may have also been developed to a certain degree. Perhaps there is something to be said for confidence. Ernest Holderness, who was a wise philosopher and co-founder of Surrey County Golf Union (in 1923) and a member of Walton Heath, and winner of the British Amateur Championship in 1922 and 1924, was able to hear firsthand, from a member of the Dunn's dynasty, the ancient golfer's belief of "the less one thinks the less chance one has of losing his/her confidence."

The action of swinging a club is so quick and so complicated, instinct has so much to do with the management of it that it is hardly possible for a golfer to explain the swing all in detail and accurately. The nervous system then added its own indignities. Holderness comments: "We cannot expect to hit the ball if we are thinking of our left hand and looking at the club-head instead of at the ball. Nothing can be more fatal than to be self-conscious when trying to play golf."

As for Aubrey Boomer, he could not claim that he understood instinctively the need for conscious control that will replace thinking, for he knew by experience that "if your golf was dependent upon thinking it was therefore at the mercy of your mental state: excitement, impulsiveness, indecision, feelings of depression, elation, any emotion could destroy you." For while a golfer might have sufficient technical skill to play a difficult shot to a very small green surrounded by bunkers (if not expertly at least adequately), the lack of control of the mental side may lead him to flub it. That is why Walter Hagen invented the phrase "smell the flowers" in order to describe the kind of peak states that keep the concentration growing while he had to go through the round without resting his attention. Flowers that no one will have the time to look at because, well, flowers are trivial and the observation of the landscape could be completely distractive.

The first great golf instructor was the ancient Greek historian Plutarch, who often quoted the Delphic oracle: "Know Yourself."

Freud and the
Uneasy Golfer's Mind

There is no evidence that Bobby Jones read Sigmund Freud. Yet in his use of the words "unconscious" and "unconsciously," Jones might have had some claim to his attention. "Unconscious" here meant "unaware," "uncomprehending," "unwitting"; this is the way the word is commonly used by Bob's contemporaries and the way it is used elsewhere in *The American Golfer* and *Golf Illustrated*. The words had been around in English since the late 17th century, and when Jones first used one of them in *The American Golfer* (September 1931), it was in a conventional and wholly un-Freudian manner. Jones concluded that a good swing depends upon the unconscious mind, for which prior mechanization is a facilitating, but not a necessary condition; the swing could go wrong the moment your conscious mind interferes with it. To be "unconscious" is simply not to notice what actually takes place as a player is swinging the club-head. But a golfer could neither pretend to be unconscious nor endeavor to take daring chances that have little hope of success. Golf is a distinctive and inspired game, and it always gives golfers a chance to make a choice. This is what Grantland Rice meant:

"The main idea in golf should be to concentrate on hitting the ball with the simplest club to get there. Any outside detail that arises to help crack or scatter concentration upon this leading essential of hitting firmly through the ball will bring about more harm than good. A golfer should play one hole at a time and in doing so maintain as much concentration and focus as possible. Good golf is a process, just one thing after another."

When the mind takes so vivid a portrait of the difficulties that beset the path, they live in it, even when the player is addressing the ball for the shot. They are very likely to cause a faltering blow, a blow born of change of intention during the swing. The task then, Bobby Jones concluded, is not to think ahead of the stroke. "Think of the right thing at the right time —and then think through the stroke. Think it over."

"Have a feeling of perfect confidence in every shot, with a foreknowledge that what has been done well once can be well repeated."

—*Glenna Collett Vare*

An Educated Habit and the Risk of Slacking Concentration

Harold Hilton supports the proposition that golfers could educate themselves into a certain spirit or philosophy. He refers to a time of "natural pugnacity" which has always served to keep him fighting to the end, and is inclined to minimize the role of imagination. As a young Hilton was not "in any way blessed with the great temperamental virtues for the playing of golf. I was extremely susceptible to the effects of outside influences and, moreover, was cursed with an imagination."

He proves the point at hand:

- It is possible to develop the habit of concentration.
- Teach yourself the skill of forgetting everything else except the particular game you are playing and the single stroke you are about to play.
- The next best thing to natural concentration is to develop the habit of continued restraint on a wandering and inconsequent brain.
- He who wins the majority of his matches is the one who starts the round trying his utmost, and continues trying until all is over.
- He who never allows the state of the match to influence his game in any way.

Alex Morrison has only one thing to say:

"Psychology, concentration, the will to win, or anything similar you care to name will not help you perform the swing correctly if you do not acquire the feel. That is why when I show you the swing in slow motion I try to describe the most vital stages in terms of what you should sense when executing the proper position and order of movements."

Nervous Jumping

For a modern golfer it is unthinkable that a man like Bobby Jones sought not to avoid anger. As he argued, anger could lead him to act completely focused and aware of what he was doing. It is part of the human condition and you have got to come to terms. If you do, you should find that anger could supply your body with extra energy. Jones appreciated this truth, all the while recognizing with mature wisdom that there is certain nervousness very useful for golf. He is supposed to have said, "Your game will never improve until you learn how to curse a little when shots go bad. We can in principle learn how to get a grip upon ourselves by cultivating concentration."

Along similar lines, Jerry Travers recounts how he had very few nervous moments in the theater of operations (the course):

"I am supposed to have nothing but ice in my veins when at play. On the contrary, I am often highly nervous and have made some of my best shots when my nerves seemed to be jumping sideways. You are not nervous, you are concentrated. Being nervous, I am a competitive golfer."

PETER DOBEREINER ON LUCK
According to Peter Dobereiner, golfers can be almost pathological about cursing their luck and blaming failure on supernatural

forces. He writes, "Some people may even convince themselves for the moment that they are indeed the victims of malicious forces. But deep inside the golfer the dreadful truth, too shaming to admit even to oneself, registers on the subconscious."[77]

---

77 Peter Dobereiner in *The Glorious World of Golf* (1973), McGraw-Hill Book Company, New York, p. 17.

Q & A

Opposing Power

Q. Why did Jim Barnes not call it concentration if you look at the ball and think about the bunker or the trap ahead?
A. Because the average duffer does not concentrate in the right way; he frequently overdoes it. Barnes was a four-time major champion, who has introspected tellingly upon the trails and the triumphs of this game. He argued that, "at least 80 percent of the golf strokes badly played are the result of breaking this concentrating effort at the vital part of the swing, which is the speed area that starts from a foot to two feet before the ball is hit. At this point, instead of thinking on through, the golfer suddenly shifts his attention to something else ahead—up goes his head—and flub goes the ball. When you are hitting the ball you have got to think about hitting the ball think all the way through about hitting the ball and think absolutely of nothing else."

"The fifth hole at Columbia (during the 1921 US Open that Barnes won) wrecked any number of scores with an out of bounds at the left of the course. Knowing this danger, when I first played this hole, I decided to investigate the right side of the hole, the safer side, to see what trouble waited for me there. I found there only average rough, not very hard to play from. So when I come to play my second shot at that hole I dismissed any thought of going out of bounds from my mind, deliberately aimed to the rough at

187

the right side and then put my entire concentration upon hitting the ball. There was no time, halfway through my swing, when I was in any doubt as to how close I was drawing the line. Aiming to the right of the course I knew that I was safe and so had nothing on my mind except swinging the club."

The result was that Barnes made par at this hole five successive times, including the qualifying rounds, while most of the other golfers took an average around 6 or 7, or even higher. He won the championship by a record margin of nine strokes.

In short, as Barnes indicates, mental control is the sort of thinking that works to the right sort of concentration. It is the foundation of correct play with every club. Without this element the rest of the game means almost nothing at all.[78]

Q. According to Vardon, what dispositions are the two enemies of correct hitting?
A. One, to have the hands slightly apart in gripping the club and, two, holding it deeply in the palms of the two hands with the knuckles well under the shaft. Vardon said, "It is an inexorable rule that, to make the ball fly straight, you must have the back of the left hand facing the way that you are going, so that it shall control the club to the extent of giving it a straight face at the impact, and that the two hands must be touching, if they are not overlapping, in order that they shall not work against one another."

Q. Why is it a "mistake" to take many balls and then putt with them up to the hole one after the other?
A. Jack White thought it was necessary to preserve an interval between putts (as there is in the real game) in order to get the full value of practice. White said, "You should take your putter and a ball onto a green where the slopes are prominent so that you may try every sort of putt that may come your way in the real

---

78 J. Lewis Brown in "Barnes Achieves the Ultimate," *Golf Illustrated*, September 1921, pp. 12, 13, 14, & 38.

game." White advised to "use only one ball, for if half a dozen or so are practiced with, you are very liable to become careless. Every practice putt should be played as if a match depended on it." He identified the best distance at which putting must be practiced and therefore the distance at which a full stroke can be gained: "Holing putts from a range of four to eight feet will give a man confidence in his methods, which is everything in golf." That sort of distance (four to eight feet from the hole) is the zone for gains, and so it should be the practice zone.

Q. According to George Duncan, which element is related (in all manner of ways) to the correct playing of games?
A. Opposed power. The quick way to good golf is thoroughly to master the principle of opposed power. Duncan intuitively knew this. He said, "We live a life of opposed power, and that does not mean frustration. Notice the difference between a boy and a girl throwing a stone. The boy intuitively pulls back vigorously the shoulder and arm opposite to the side from which he throws; invariably, the girl lets the opposite side 'go' with the one from which she throws, with 'empty' results. Golf is played exactly as the boy throws the stone. That weight of yours must oppose the movement of the club both in the backswing and at the moment of impact between the club-head and ball. The follow-through ought to come automatically."

Q. What is the reason that Harold Hilton said "It is bad for a golfer to anticipate the play and possible difficulties to be over-come in every hole on the way round"?
A. Whoever imagines how a particular difficulty would be over-come at the 15th or 16th whole while playing, say, the third hole, is thinking ahead of time, puzzling problems for the future which might never happen. Hilton said, "To this day if I still find my attention wandering away ahead of schedule, I have to pull myself up sharply." He considered this a curse of an unduly antic-ipatory brain. He added, "I find the greatest difficulty in reining it in, from participating in the many imaginative pictures which

it will persist in weaving. A persistent and anticipatory brain of an imaginative character is an ill possession for a golfer to be blessed with."

"In a game both sides strive to get the verdict, but the verdict is not really important; it is the striving which makes the game worth the energy expended."

—John Laing Low

Develop Courage

By Walter Hagen

To become a great golfer one must acquire something more than the knowledge of how to make shots. It happens frequently that a poor player comes out on top in match play because he often possesses more bull dog courage than his opponent with a better game. My advice to anyone who wants to learn golf is to develop courage along with the science of swinging the clubs. I know of no better way than to play in stiff competition whenever the chance offers. Try to get in a game where your opponents are better players, even if you must accept odds that look humiliating. You will learn the fine points of the game much more quickly this way than you will by engaging in golf with weaker opponents where little or no effort is required to win. There are a lot of players who have rooms full of golf trophies that they have won from inferior players. For the good of one's game it would be better to lose every round to a good golfer than it would be to win every time from a poor player.[79]

"There is one thing that has helped me more in match play than any other factor, and that is to play each shot by itself. This faculty didn't come naturally or easily. It came only through hard practice and concentration."

—Jerry Travers

---

79 Walter Hagen in "Courage Counts in Golf," *Golfers Magazine*, April 1928.

Tips to Improve the Mental Side

By Jim Barnes

WHEN YOU COME UP TO THE BALL

- First you must decide firmly and definitely what club you need to reach the green.
- Then, in taking your stance, be sure of the right line of play.
- Don't wait, halfway through the swing, to wonder whether you are aiming too far to the right or to the left, whether you should have used a mashie in place of a jigger, or a spoon in place of an iron.
- Have all that definitely located before you start your backswing.
- Once you've decided, then you have but one job left: to put your entire mind on hitting that golf ball with the best swing you have to use.
- Don't trouble yourself with keeping your eye on the ball. If you are thinking about the ball all the way through your swing, you are most certainly going to look at it.
- Just keep your mind there and your eye will be there too.

Unless you make a practice of correct thinking, of making mind and muscle work together, of concentration upon the swing alone, you are not going to get very far. It may not come too easy at first, but it will make all the difference in the world in your game.[80]

---

80 James Barnes in "Tips to Improve the Mental Side; Q & A—The First Thing to Learn," *The American Golfer*, New York, August 27, 1921, pp. 3 & 28.

The Why Questions

Why did Roger Wethered say that golf is an exception to the saying that the bad workman blames his tools? Because poor clubs will have a disastrous effect on any player's game: "they may easily cause radical alterations in the swing itself," Roger said, "and when all is said and done, the golf swing is such a susceptible organism that it is liable to conform to the imperfections of the instruments."

Why did Grantland Rice have to say that the temperament for winning golf is quite different from the temperament needed for tennis or football? To state that golf calls for a greater ability to concentrate, for greater repression. "Golf requires great control over the emotional or nervous system," he said. "Where the tendency in football, tennis and such is to leap forward, the tendency in golf should be to restrain over-eagerness and impetuous action."

Why did Percy Boomer talk about "the down feeling at the top of the backswing"? Because golfers should keep their arms in front of them and down as they rotate the shoulders on the backswing. To hit the ball the arms should not lift up in the air independent of the pivot. It is forbidden to lock the left elbow straight at the top of the backswing. In the down feeling, the arms should be leveraged against the body to gain power and consistent golf swing.

Why did Travis say that looking up is not so much the cause of a terrible shot as it is the moving of the head from the horizontal (in other words, raising it vertically)? To teach us that the head is not at fault more than the eye. "Keep the head in the same horizontal plane throughout," he said, "and there will be few mistakes. Lift it vertically and anything may happen." For Harvey Penick, looking up is the "biggest alibi ever invented" to explain a bad shot. "By the time you look up, you've already made the mistake that caused the bad shot," he said. When Harvey told a student to keep his eye on the ball, it was usually to give him something to think about that won't do any harm. Penick states: "I've known only three or four top players who say they actually see the ball when they hit it. Even Ben Hogan told me he loses sight of the ball 'somewhere in my downswing.'"

Why does a golf instructor have to tell the pupil to keep his left arm straight? To suggest that in order to keep the club well away from the body in the early part of the upswing and to prevent the novice from adopting that "wrong way to do it," pictures of which show the player with the club wrapped around his neck. When the pro said, "keep your left arm straight," he knows that it would bend slightly at the top of the swing but thought it safer not to tell the player so.

A bluffed duffer once told Stuart Maiden that he was hooking one shot and slicing the next. "Why not try topping a few?" was the expert advice awarded on the spot.

The Most Difficult Shot

By Francis Ouimet

Reiterating a conviction he had stated in his early collection of essays for *The American Golfer*, where he spoke of the "lazy mental attitude" on the first tee as a great idea though few can follow any such course with the lure of the fairway up ahead, Francis Ouimet said in 1932:

"There is something really awful about the tee-shot from the first teeing-ground on a Saturday morning. The average member of any club knows that in all probability the eyes of a large number of his friends are fastened upon him and that to fail will bring forth a few uncomplimentary remarks from his fellow players.

"I saw Walter Hagen once in a Massachusetts Open Championship, which he won, top his tee-shot from the first teeing-ground so badly that it did not cover 20 yards and ended up in the muddy racetrack in front of the tee. But Hagen was not altogether to blame, for as he was starting the downswing his foot slipped and he did well to hit the ball at all. However, the crowd failed to notice Walter's misfortune, and all they could think of was the wretched shot he made.

"If the process of hitting the first drive at the first tee is worth attention, so is its psychology. . . . 'I have heard of cases where you cannot feel the club on your hands,' Hagen said. Well when he got on the first teeing ground he could not feel that their legs were on the ground—much less the club in the hands. Agony claws the mind, he is paralyzed. Then, the ball is addressed and it suddenly seemed to disappear. He doesn't know what happened, but somebody said, 'Good shot!' He has no idea where the ball had gone, but allows the caddie to lead him to it."

Play Your Own Game

By Francis Ouimet

The golfer, to be successful, must first know just what he can and cannot do with each club in his bag. He should not try to follow the example of his opponent, no matter how brilliant that opponent may be. I am quite sure that my good friend Jerry Travers would [never] have been such a wonderful golfer had he attempted to imitate the play of many of his opponents during the big matches he so frequently won. Time and again Jerry would face players who obtained distances from the tee with the wood but when Jerry could not get his wood going well, he never fell into the trap of trying to match them stroke for stroke, even though their drives were splendid ones. Jerry would play the game as he knew he could play it. He simply knew what he could do with each club in his bag. He was never concerned with what other stars could do with such and such a club. That was the dominating factor in his success, just as it is the dominating factor in the ranking of any fine golfer.

One day in 1913 I was facing the biggest event of my golf days. As a boy, I had tied Vardon and Ray, the English professionals, in the United States Open, at 72 holes of medal play. The following day we played off this tie. I had played the course several times in fine figures and realized all that. But as the time for the start began, my case seemed hopeless to me. Then, as I was about to

198

tee up, little Johnny McDermott, the greatest professional player we ever developed in America, came to me and said, "Play your own game, Francis." Suddenly it came to me that here was the secret of golf. So I set forth with new resolve. My mind was given entirely to my own game. I forgot about Vardon and Ray, and set to work to play the best golf of which I was capable. And the best part of it all is that I succeeded in doing so.[81]

81 "Avoid Imitation in Golf," *St. Nicholas: An Illustrated Magazine for Boys and Girls*, Volume 47, 1920, pp. 981–884.

Retelling Francis Ouimet's Victory at the 1913 US Open in Brookline

By John G. Anderson

It was 1913. Born and bred in Brookline, Massachusetts, Francis DeSales Ouimet was working at a neighborhood sports store. He had qualified to compete in the US Open through his victory in the Amateur Championship of Massachusetts. He was still in his teens and he was not considered a great player. But he had grown up right across the street from the Country Club of Brookline, where the Open would be played. By contrast, Harry Vardon and Edward Ray were the best players in the world. They had the experience the local youngest lacked. This is how John G. Anderson remembered this Open[82]:

Vardon, Ray, Reid, and Tellier had set the pace early in the play, had been caught at the various times by at least a half dozen American golfers, but, starting out on the last round were in a tie at 225 only with Ouimet who was expected to fade from the picture. (During the last round) when Ray went to the turn in 43 and Vardon in 42 there was little help left in them; Tellier killed his hopes with two 6s on the first five holes coming home, blotted out international success with Francis as the victor.

---

82 John G. Anderson in "The Greatest Golf Finish I Ever Saw," *The American Golfer*, May 7, 1921, pp. 6 & 34.

[Francis], who went out in 43, was left with the seemingly impossible task of making the last six holes in 22, bogey (sic) for which as the card indicated was 26 in order to tie the English golfers. The 15th hole borders on the clubhouse grounds and there came pouring forth 5,000 spectators idly curious in most respects. They saw nothing to startle them, for Ouimet's drive was sliced and his second shot was 40 yards from the hole with two intervening traps. I was immediately back of Ouimet when he made his approach shot and I consider it the second best shot in golf I have ever seen. To begin with, no ball pitched two feet over the traps could be held near the cup. The ball had to strike within six inches of the trap's edge to permit of the lessening run and a windup near the cup. To make matters more difficult, Ouimet had been approaching with a mashie not laid back any too deep making the stroke ten times more severe. But he brought off the shot with a perfection to detail which has always remained in my memory. His putt of a yard he made simple.

Ouimet needed a 3 on the 360-yards 17th to tie the score at that point of Vardon and Ray. His drive was good; his approach six yards past the cup brought a smile to the face of his mother, watching from the wall at the back of the green. Jerome Travers had a grip of my shoulder and I knew once more where the strength came from, which had helped to win his fourth amateur championship at Garden City two weeks before.

"Ten dollars he holds it!" said Travers. Of course the putt went down. That is history. In years to come it will become more famous. Not a soul who witnessed it, including Vardon and Ray, will ever forget it. The last hole, so far as the gallery goes, was played for Ouimet long before he stepped to the tee. A drive, a long approach, a run-up putt and then, well, there were a few shivers when the young lad stepped up to a three-foot putt and without sighting from front or back hit the ball into the cup for the very 22 for six holes that was needed and a tie with Vardon and Ray, a tie for America. The play next day to me seemed like an anticlimax. The game was won on the 69th and 71st holes.

Golf Proverbs

By Alfred W. Tillinghast

He cannot be a good player who knows not why he is good.

* * * * *

The worst part of a bad round is to bear it impatiently.

* * * * *

Lying golfers begin by imposing on others, but end by deceiving themselves.

* * * * *

Better conquer a hole than always fear it.

* * * * *

To believe a shot impossible is the sure way to make it so.

* * * * *

Though your adversity seems a mouse, watch him like a lion.

* * * * *

A good round needs no explanation and a bad one deserves none.

* * * * *

Bad players excuse their faults; good ones quit them.

* * * * *

Golf is a mirror, in which we see the best and worst of ourselves.

* * * * *

It is easier to learn good strokes than to correct bad ones.

* * * * *

Why compare bad courses? There is small choice in rotten apples.

* * * * *

There is a little to choose between greens at night.

* * * * *

The worst hazard on any course is a garrulous companion.

* * * * *

By ignorance we mistake and by mistakes we learn.

* * * * *

The end of a bad round is the beginning of humility.

* * * * *

Never make a mountain of a molehill or tee-sand.

* * * * *

Real golf, like coral, needs no coloring.

* * * * *

By observing other's faults, some golfers correct their own. By watching correct golf, faults are corrected more easily.

* * * * *

Care killed the cat, and over-care kills many a score.

* * * * *

There are golfers who, like cuckoos, have but one song—"My own game."

* * * * *

Out to the pit and into the cup is like killing two flies with one swat.

* * * * *

It is a stupid mouse that knows only one hole. (And the man who plays only one course is a lost soul when he tackles another.)

* * * * *

No relying on wine, women, and putters.

* * * * *

"It is Chinese grammar to us." (So are the rules of golf to some.)

* * * * *

True golfers, unlike stymies, are not measured by inches.

* * * * *

A fine club, in the hands of a dub, is a crow-bar.

* * * * *

The word "impossible" is not in any true golfer's dictionary.

* * * * *

Slicing is the score's sepulcher.

* * * * *

Let Mahomet be your ball, and the cup the mountain.

* * * * *

Knowledge without practice makes but half a golfer.

* * * * *

Beating from good players is better than always licking dubs.

* * * * *

A good green on a bad hole is like a diamond necklace about a sow's neck.

* * * * *

It is the sign of a great golfer if he grows better for commendation.

* * * * *

The dub finds consolation in the thought that his game can't get worse.

* * * * *

Poor shots may be cured, but there is no medicine for fear.

* * * * *

Bad shots are soon learned.

* * * * *

An old ball, like an old umbrella, is seldom lost.

* * * * *

He conquers twice who conquers himself in victory.

* * * * *

The angry golfer opens his mouth and shuts his eyes.

* * * * *

Creator of Golf Courses

Founder of the PGA of America, Albert Warren (A. W.) Tillinghast was at the luncheon in 1916 when Rodman Wanamaker wanted to form an organization for American professionals. It is claimed that he helped invent the word "birdie" with a group of buddies while golfing at Atlantic City Country Club. He became the Patron Saint of the USGA Green Section when he advocated for turf grass research, and during the Great Depression, he fought for lowing the cost of golf and raising maintenance standards. He wrote: "It must be remembered that the great majority of golfers are aiming to reduce their previous best performance by five strokes if possible, first, last, and all the time, and if any one of them arrives at the home teeing ground with this possibility in reach, he is not caring two hoots whether he is driving off from nearby an ancient oak of majestic size and form or a dead sassafras. If his round ends happily it is one beautiful course. Such is human nature."[83]

---

83 Quoted by Geoff Shackelford in *Golf Digest* online, October 16, 2014: http://www.golfdigest.com/story/hall-of-fame-aw-tillinghast

Acknowledgments

I am indebted to Jerry Tarde, chairman and editor in chief of Golf Digest companies, and to Robert Rinner, CEO of *Golf Illustrated*. Tarde, on behalf of Conde Nast, has provided permission to reprint timeless stories, lessons, and teachings from *The American Golfer* magazine, which was acquired by Conde Nast in 1928. This book would not have found its present form without their permission to quote freely from both magazines. These important texts were the most relevant to learn the game in the roaring twenties. A huge, huge thanks goes out to Cliff Schrock, editor of Golf Digest Resource Center. Cliff has supplied the photographic material. My agent, Maryann Karinch, encouraged me when this book was nothing but a half-baked conjecture, insisting that I keep going. I've also benefited from the feedback of many friends and colleagues. I'd like to especially thank David H. Clarke, Bradley Klein, Art Spander, Curt Sampson, and Fr. Thomas Gallagher. They enriched my insight. I was so lucky to have them on my side.

List of Contributors

Tommy Dickson Armour (1894–1968) Born in Edinburgh, the Silver Scot was the third of only nine golfers in history to win the US Open (1927), the British Open (1931), and the PGA Championship (1930). He won three Canadian Opens as well as 24 other events in the United States.

Glenna Collett Vare (1903–1989) She was a pioneer in American women's golf and a Hall of Fame golfing champion who dominated American women's golf in the 1920s, winning six US Women Amateur Championships, two Canadian Ladies Opens, and the French Ladies Open. She was known as the female Bobby Jones.

Henry Cotton (1907–1987) He was an English pro. He won three British Championships and 11 national championships on the continent of Europe. He authored ten books, designed golf courses, and was the most respected and prolific British instructor of his era. His philosophy was simple: "To be a champion, you must act like one."

Bobby Cruickshank (1894–1975) He was a Scottish pro who won 17 tour events in his career, including the Los Angeles and Texas Opens in 1927, and finished as the leading money winner for the year. He had 16 top-ten finishes (nine top-six) in major championships. The closest he came to the elusive big one was twice being runner-up at the US Open, in 1923 and 1932.

Bernard Darwin (1876–1961) He was the most revered writer in golf. A grandson of the British naturalist Charles Darwin, he was a prominent authority on Charles Dickens and editor of *The Oxford Dictionary of Quotations.*

Peter Dobereiner (1926–1996) He was a golfer and correspondent of both the *London Observer* and the *Guardian.* He wrote a column for *Golf Digest* magazine from 1973 to 1996, and was the author of 27 books. He absorbed the wisdom of the greatest golf architects and became a course designer himself.

Vivian Doran She was born in Canada and was a member of the Ingersoll Golf & Country Club in London, Ontario. She wrote for *The American Golfer* during the 1920s.

John Duncan Dunn (1874–1951) He was a course designer and teacher. He wrote many magazine articles and several books, including *Natural Golf* in 1931. He was the scion of a famous golfing family, his great-uncle Willie being one of the "Dunnies" who played in high-wager matches against Old Tom Morris and Alan Robertson.

James Douglas Edgar (1884–1921) Born in Newcastle, England, he won the Canadian Open in 1919 and 1920, and the French Open in 1914. He lost to Jock Hutchinson in the match play final of the PGA in 1920. He was an innovator and mentor to Bobby Jones. Steve Eubanks described him as the father of the modern swing, who was the first to employ many of the principles considered to be fundamental in later years.

Charles Evans Jr. (1890–1979) He was the first amateur to win the United States Amateur and the United States Open in one year (1916). He played in 50 consecutive United States Amateurs, winning again in 1920.

Johnny Farrell (1901–1988) For two years (1927 and 1928) he was voted Best Golf Professional of the Year after winning eight consecutive tournaments, including the 1928 US Open. Farrell left the tour in 1934 to become a resident professional at Baltusrol Golf Club. He had won a total of 22 events.

Harold Hilton (1869–1942) He was an English amateur. He won the Open Championship in 1892 and 1897. He also won The British Amateur Championship four times, including 1911, when he became the first British player to win the British and US Amateurs in the same year.

Ernest Holderness (1890–1968) In full Sir Ernest William Elsmie Holderness, he was an English amateur and golf philosopher. He won the British Amateur Championship in 1922 and 1924. From 1933 to 1939, he handled much of the policy work at the Aliens Department of the Home Office, responsible for dealing with the mass of refugees from Nazism.

Bobby Jones (1902–1971) The greatest amateur golfer ever; he won 13 major championships between 1923 and 1930, before retiring from the game at age 28 in 1930. Then he went on to help design the Augusta National, the site of the Masters.

Ernest Jones (1887–1965) He was a scholarly English pro and instructor who, in the fifties, probably conducted more lessons than any other instructor in the game. He lost his right leg in World War I and broke par on championship courses while balanced on his left foot.

Oscar Bane Keeler (1882–1950) He was, in the words of Bobby Jones, "the greatest golf writer who ever lived." He chronicled every tournament ever played by Jones. And he also functioned as his friend, mentor, biographer, and press agent. As a veteran *Atlanta Journal* sports staffer, he won national recognition as a writer and authority on golf.

Henry Longhurst (1909–1978) He was for decades Britain's voice of golf with his distinguished commentaries on the sport in

Golf Illustrated from 1954 to 1969. For 45 years he was also correspondent of the *Sunday Times* of London. He also announced for CBS from the Masters tournament for eight years, covering the 16th hole.

Steward Maiden (1886–1948) He was one of the best known Carnoustie teachers. According to Bobby Jones, his distinguished pupil, he had "the finest and soundest style I have ever seen. I grew up swinging like him. I imitated his style, like a monkey."

Alex J. Morrison He was a golf instructor and was one of four brothers who were all golf professionals back in the 1920s throughout the 1950s. From 1932 to 1940 he published three books, one of which was the foundations of modern golf instruction: *A New Way to Better Golf* (1932). He taught Henry Picard and Horton Smith.

Francis Ouimet (1893–1967) He was an American golf prodigy and pioneer. His "Cinderella" victory in the 1913 US Open is considered possibly the most important moment in American golf history. He won the US Amateur in 1914 and 1931, and the French Amateur Championship in 1914. He became the first America to be selected as captain of the R&A in 1951.

Willie Park (1864–1925) He was a British professional born in Scotland and winner of the Open Championship twice (1887 and 1889). He was arguably the finest putter that British golf has ever produced. Park, who was also a successful golf writer and course designer, took up permanent residence in the United States in 1916.

Grantland Rice (1880–1954) Henry Grantland Rice was a sports columnist and author who established himself over many years as one of the US's leading sports authorities, for whom golf was fundamentally an art. He would go onto to mythologize the sport heroes of the Golden Age of American sports of the twenties and eventually served as editor of *The American Golfer* between November 1918 and 1936.

Gene Sarazen (1902–1999) Born Eugenio Saraceni, he won 39 PGA Tournaments, including seven major championships. He was the first man to achieve the modern Grand Slam: US Open, British Open, PGA, and Masters (other winners are Ben Hogan, Gary Player, Jack Nicklaus, and Tiger Woods).

Phillips B. Thompson He was a regular contributor of *Golf Illustrated*. He authored the book *Simplifying the Golf Stroke*, published by L. Gomme in 1929. It was a small text of only 15 pages, based on the theory of Ernest Jones.

Albert Warren Tillinghast (1876–1942) He was a course architect, perhaps the greatest in the history of golf. He was 41 years old when he began his distinctive career by designing the San Francisco Golf Club in 1915. Among his masterpieces we can include Bethpage State Park Black Course (1935), Somerset Hills (1918), the 36 holes each at Winged Foot (1923) and Baltusrol (1922), Ridgewood Country Club (1929), and Quaker Ridge Golf Club (1926).

Jerry Travers (1887–1951) Inspired by Ouimet's victory, he became the second amateur to win the US Open in 1915. He won the Open at Baltusrol after taking four US Amateur titles and five Metropolitan Amateurs. He was known as the best match player in the 1910s.

Walter Travis (1862–1927) Born in Maldon, Australia, he came to the United States in 1886, and later became an American citizen. He bought his first set of golf clubs at the age of 34. He won the US National Amateur Champion in 1990, 1901, and 1904, and the Britain Amateur Championship at Sandwich in 1903. He was a golf journalist and publisher (founding *The American Golfer* magazine in 1908), turf-grass expert, and one of the great golf course architects. His career ended at age 53 by winning the Metropolitan Amateur in New York.

Percy Adolphus Vaile (1866–1940) He was a prolific writer on golf and tennis. He practiced law in his native New Zealand and was also active as an inventor of golf and tennis equipment and of marine and aviation devices. He was the author of *Modern Golf; Modern Lawn Tennis; Swerve, or the Flight of the Ball*; and *The Soul of Golf*.

Cyril Walker (1892–1948) Born in Manchester, UK, he emigrated to the United States in 1914. Playing out of Englewood Golf Club in New Jersey, he won the 28th US Open at Oakland Hills Country Club in 1924. He won the Indiana Open in 1926 and six PGA tournaments from 1917 to 1930. He died of pleural pneumonia in a Hackensack, New Jersey jail cell, where he had gone for shelter.

Douglas B. Wesson (1884–1956) He was the author of *I'll Never Be Cured and I Don't Much Care: The History of an Acute Attack of Golf and Pertinent Remarks Relating to Various Places of Treatment*, published in 1928. He was born in Springfield, Massachusetts, and was the author of numerous articles in *Golf Illustrated*.

Joyce Wethered (1901–1997) She won the British Ladies Amateur four times (1922, 1924, 1925, and 1929) and the English Ladies' champion for five consecutive years (1920–24). She was the Queen of British amateur golf. Willie Wilson, the Scottish pro, said that "She could hit a ball 240 yards on the fly while standing barefoot on a cake of ice."

Roger Henry Wethered (1899–1983) He was an English amateur golfer who was the brother of Joyce. He tied for the British Open title in 1921 but lost the playoff to Jock Hutchison. But he got the amateur records for the Old Course with 72 and 71 in the third and fourth rounds. He won the British Amateur Champion in 1923; he was runner-up in 1928 and 1930.

References

Anderson, John: "The Greatest Golf Finish I Ever Saw," *The American Golfer*, May 7, 1921, pages 6 & 34; "The Lure of Length," *The American Golfer*, January 14, 1922, pages 10 & 22.

Armour, Tommy: "The Speed Area, Tips Worth Taking," *The American Golfer*, October 22, 1921, Volume XXII, No. 21, page 4.

Barnes, Jim: "How Is Your Slice?," *The American Golfer*, January 28, 1922, pages 4 & 30.

Braid, James: "Braid on Long Driving," *The American Golfer*, October 1916, Volume 16, No. 6, pp. 449 & 450; "Tips to Improve the Mental Side; Q & A—The First Thing to Learn," *The American Golfer*, August 27, 1921, Volume XXIV, pages 3 & 28; "The Wisdom of Braid," *The American Golfer*, August 1916, Volume 16, No. 4, pages 269–272.

Brown, J. Lewis: "Barnes Achieves The Ultimate," *Golf Illustrated*, September 1921, pp. 12, 13, 14 & 38.

Burke, James Francis: "Our Bobby," *Golf Illustrated*, August 1926, page 22.

Cruickshank, Bobby: "Playing the Long Iron," *The American Golfer*, September 8, 1923, Volume 26, Issue 18, pages 11 & 40.

Darwin, Bernard: "The Eye on the Ball," *The American Golfer*, October 6, 1923, Volume 26, No. 20, page 19; "Keeping the Body Still," *Golf Illustrated*, June 1920, pages 12, 13, 44, & 46; "To Think or Not to Think," *The American Golfer*, December 13, 1924, Volume 27, Issue 25, pages 9 & 30; "The Useful Art of Recovery," *The American Golfer*, February 1928, pages 17 & 42; "Wrists—Flexible or Stiff in Putting?" *The American Golfer*, October 20, 1923, pages 7 & 29.

Doran, Vivian: "The Art of Sound Putting," *The American Golfer*, April 22, 1922, pages 8, 9, & 26; "Cheating the Wind, Along the Fairways," *The*

Lewiston Daily Sun, April 12, 1928; "The Putting Touch," *The American Golfer*, December 30, 1922, page 7.

Duncan, George: "How I Cure Faults," *The American Golfer*, January 14, 1920, pages 6, 28, & 29; "The Methods of Champions, Comparing the Swings of Famous British Professionals in Executing a Full Shot," *The American Golfer*, January 28, 1922, pages 13 & 36; "Settling the Confusion: Left or Right Hand? Left Hand Control Again!" *Golf Illustrated*, February 1933, pages 14 & 15.

Duncan Dunn, John: "American and British Thought on Golf," *Golf Illustrated*, November 1932, pages 20, 21 & 39; *Intimate Golf Talks* (1920), G. P. Putnam's Sons, London, UK; "American and British Thought on Golf—I," *Golf Illustrated*, November 1932, pages 20, 21, & 39; "Conscious Control and the Lofting Shot," *Golfers Magazine*, Volume 36, No. 3, March, 1920, pages 17 & 20.

Farrell, Johnny: "The Chip Shot," *Golf Illustrated*, October 1927, Volume 28, Issue 1, page 15; "Golfers Who Bloom in the Spring," *Golf Illustrated*, May 1934, page 19; "You Win When You Least Expect To," *The American Golfer*, August 1928, pages 8 & 57.

Hagen, Walter: "Begin with the Putter, Then Take Up the Mashie, the Brassie," *Golfers Magazine*, May 1922, pages 31 & 60; "The Club That Gets There," *The American Golfer*, April 3, 1920, Volume 23, Issue 6, pages 11 & 38; "Courage Counts in Golf," *Golfers Magazine*, April 1928 "Seven Resolutions," *Golfers Magazine*, January 1924; "Some of Them Will Go Wrong," *The American Golfer*, June 1926, Volume 29, Issue 9, pages 31 & 70.

Hannigan, Frank: "A. W. Tillinghast, His Life and Work," By Frank Hannigan, *The Golf Journal*, May 1974, pages 14–28.

Hilton, Harold: "Be Up," *The American Golfer*, January 1926, Volume 29, Issue 4, pages 17 & 38, by special arrangement with *London Golf Illustrated*; "Can We Over-Concentrate?" *Golf Illustrated*, July 30, 1926; "Has Golf Improved?" *Golf Illustrated* & *Outdoor America*, April 1914, Volume 1, issue 1, pages 13–15; "How It Feels to Be a Champion," *The American Golfer*, February 1927, Volume 30, Issue 5, pages 9 & 39; "Jerome Travers Makes Good", *Golf Illustrated* & *Outdoor America*, August 1915, Volume 3, Issue 5, pages 50, 52, & 54; "Practice in Golf, The Value of Consistent Training to Beginners and Others," *Outing Magazine*, Volume LX, Issue 5, August 1912, page 597; "Talking Your Opponent Off His Game," *Golf Illustrated*, February 1928, pages 13, 39, & 40, by special arrangement with *London Golf Illustrated*; "Why Vardon Never Left a Divot," *Golf Illustrated*, August 16, 1935.

Holderness, Sir Ernest: "The Angle of Striking," *The American Golfer*, April 1930, page 29.

Jones, Bobby (Robert Tyre Jones Jr.): "Answering Oft-Asked Questions," *Golf Illustrated*, October 1928, pages 14 & 15; "Bobby Jones Names Six Fundamentals," *The American Golfer*, April 1932, page 9; "Concerning the Pendulum Stroke in Putting," *The American Golfer*, March 1930; "How to Save Strokes," *The American Golfer*, August 1934, Volume 37, Issue 11, pages 9 & 52; "On Concentration," *The American Golfer*, August 1935, pages 19 & 37; "The Pressure of The Open," *The American Golfer*, June 1932, pages 11 & 53.

Jones, Ernest: "Cause and Effect in the Golf Swing," *Golf Illustrated*, March 1931, pages 19 & 51; "The Fundamentals of Swing and Grip," *Golf Illustrated*, February 1933, pages 24, 25, & 34; "Good Golf Is Easy No. 6," *The American Golfer*, January 1935, page 18; "Hit with the Club-Head," *The American Golfer*, July 1927, Volume 30, Issue 10, pages 27 & 52; "Mastering the Control," *The American Golfer*, December 1929, page 11.

Keeler, O. B.: "'Form' and 'Style'," *The American Golfer*, February 11, 1922, pages 13 & 24; "Hit It at Something!," *The American Golfer*, March 11, 1922, Volume 25, No. 5, pages 15, 30, & 31; "How Bobby Jones Started," *The American Golfer*, June 5, 1920, pages 4, 5, & 25; "It Is All Between the Ears," *The American Golfer*, December 1927, pages 17 & 35; "Look to Your Pivoting: Stewart Maiden Claims a Good Deal Turns on This Phase of the Swing," *The American Golfer*, April 8, 1922, Volume XXV, Number 7, pages 5 & 24; "Set the Mind to Watch the Mind," *The American Golfer*, August 11, 1923; "'Shoot the Works,' Says Stewart Maiden," *The American Golfer*, December 27, 1924, Volume 27, Issue 26, pages 3 & 29; "A Tale of Two Champions, Harry Vardon & Bobby Jones," *The American Golfer*, May 2, 1925; "When You Shoot Your Very Best Rounds," *The American Golfer*, May 20, 1922, Volume 25, pages 14 & 27.

Leach, Henry: "Glances Upon American Golf History (Part I)," *The American Golfer*, February 1918, Volume 19, No. 4, pages 439–445; "The Great Shots of Golf," *The American Golfer*, December 1914, Volume 13, No. 2, pages 102–109; "The Human Vardon," *The American Golfer*, January 1917, Volume 17, No. 3, pages 172–192; "The Language of Golf," *The American Golfer*, April 1918, Volume 19, No. 6, pages 567–574; "The Lonely Putter," *The American Golfer*, August 1918, Volume 20, No. 4, pages 847–852; "Ouimet Explained," *The American Golfer*, August 1916, Volume 16, No. 4, pages 252–266; "Philosophy and Golf," *The American Golfer*, April 1917, Volume 17, No. 6, pages 445–465; "Players of the Period—VIII: Mr. Jerome D. Travers," *The American Golfer*, March 1916, Volume 15, No. 5, pages 310–324; "The Scientific Hilton," *The American Golfer*, December 1916, Volume 17, No. 2, pages 86 & 103; "The Training of Travis," *The American Golfer*, May 1917, Volume 18, No. 1, pages 539–559.

Leitch, Cecil: "Common Faults," *Golf Illustrated*, September 1921, page 22.

Longhurst, Henry: *About Walter Hagen, On Golf And Life* (1979), compiled & edited by Mark Wilson and Ken Bowden, Collins, St. James's Place, London, UK, pages 67–72.

Morrison, Alex J.: "By Sight or Feel," *The American Golfer*, September 1932, Volume 35, Issue 12, pages 19 & 40; "The Three Sources of Freedom," *The American Golfer*, April 1929, Volume 32, Issue 7, pages 18, 19, & 54; "The Unconscious Golfer," *The American Golfer*, May 1932, pages 17 & 55.

Ouimet, Francis: "Avoid Imitation in Golf," *St. Nicolas: An Illustrated Magazine for Boys and Girls,* September 1920, Volume XLVII, pages 981–984; "Close to the Flag," *Golf Illustrated,* November 1926, Volume 26, No. 2, pages 17 & 45; "Suggestions for Putting," *Golf Illustrated & Outdoor America,* April 1914, Volume I, Issue 1, pages 16 & 17; "Teaching My Wife to Play Golf," *The American Golfer,* October 22, 1921, Volume XXII, No. 21, pages 3, 26, 27, & 28; "Winning the Open," *The American Golfer,* July 1913, Volume 10, No. 3, pages 590 & 594.

Park, William Jr.: "The Art of Putting," *The American Golfer,* February 12, 1921, pages 4 & 28; "On Putting," *The American Golfer,* December 1916, Volume 17, No. 2, pages 104 & 105.

Perkins, T. Philip: "Simplifying the Judgment of Distance," *Golf Illustrated,* March 1931.

Rice, Grantland/*The American Golfer*: "Another Way to Save Strokes," April 10, 1920, page 19; "Applying a Winning Tip," August 1923, Volume 36, Issue 8, pages 24; "The Essential Ingredient," April 24, 1920, Volume 23, Issue 9, pages 13 & 23; "The Golfing Drama of Male and Female," December 3 1921, Volume 4, Issue 24, pages 7 & 30; "How Hagen Putts," April 21, 1922, Volume 26, No. 8, pages 7 & 36; "Interviewing Alex Morrison," February 1933, pages 7 & 37; "Making it Tougher for Yourself," July 20, 1920, page 15; "The Marvel of Walter J. Travis," September 1927, pages 11 & 39; "Match Play Masters," October 20, 1923, pages 8 & 28; "The Most Important Stroke," March 1927, pages 11 & 40; "Ready to Hit the Ball," April 22, 1922, Volume 25, No. 8, pages 5 & 26; "A Simple Stroke Worth Learning," May 21, 1921, Volume 24, Issue 10, pages 13 & 32; "The Temperament for Winning Golf," February 11, 1922, pages 5 & 32; "Tips worth Taking," October 22, 1921, Volume XXII, N 21, page 4; "What is Your Favorite Fault?" April 9, 1921, Volume 24, Issue 7, pages 11 & 21; "What Your Game Needs Most," November 5, 1921, Volume 24, Issue 22, pages 5 & 26; "Which is the Hitting Arm in Golf?" June 5, 1920, Volume 23, Issue 15, pages 11 & 27; "Why Good Golf is Hard to Learn," March 24, 1923, Volume 26, Issue 6, Page 15.

Rice, Jack: "The Worst Fault in Golf Is Dead Hands," *The American Golfer,* 1932.

Sarazen, Gene: "The Door to the Cup," *The American Golfer,* January 1925, Volume 28, Issue 1, pages 30 & 39; "We Must Avoid Playing Safe: Golf Medicine from Master Doctors," *The American Golfer,* October 20, 1923, page 22.

Sherlock, J. in "Temperament and Other Matters That May, or May Not, Help One's Game," *Golf, USGA, Bulletin,* February 1917, pp. 85–89.

Thompson, Phillips B.: "Hands and the Club-Head," *Golf Illustrated,* August 1931, page 48.

Travers, Jerry: "Bring the Club Back—Slowly, a Former Champion Recalls," *The American Golfer,* June 1933, pages 25 & 44; "Chipped Approaches," *Golf Illustrated,* September 1933, page 23; "The Drive," *The American Golfer,*

June 1913, Volume 10, Issue 2, pages 99–107; "Modern Golf," annotated by Walter J. Travis, *The American Golfer*, March 1909, Volume 1, Issue 5 pages 229–234; "Think Before You Putt," *The American Golfer*, March 1933, Volume 36, Issue 6, pages 21 & 42;

Travis, Walter/*The American Golfer:* "Building up a Game, IV–Iron-Clubs" August 21, 1920, Volume 23, Issue 26, page 11; "How to Putt," March 1911, Volume 5, No. 5, pages 367–370; "The Left Side," In conversation with Grantland Rice; quoted in "Why Good Golf is Hard to Learn, by Grantland Rice," March 24, 1923, Volume 26, Issue 6, page 15; "Modern Golf," March 1909, Volume 1, No. 5, pages 229–234/April 1909, Volume 1, No. 6, pages 293–299; "The Origin of the Schenectady Putter," written by B. B. H, March, 1911, Volume 5, No. 5 pages 371 & 372; "Tabloid Tips," August 1919, page 782; "Twenty Years of Golf," August 14, 1920, Volume 23, Issue 25, pages 15–20/August 28, Volume 23, Issue 27, pages 9 & 19.

Vaile, P. A.: "Can a Man Improve His Golf After Forty?" *Golf, USGA Bulletin*, February 1917, pp. 73–78; "Observations on Diegel's Putting," *Golf Illustrated*, March 1931, pages 34, 35, & 52.

Vardon, Harry: "Bunker Philosophy and Practice," *The American Golfer*, February 1918, Volume 19, Issue 4, pages 446–451; "The Driving Swing," *Golf Illustrated*, November 1921, Volume 16, Issue 2, pages 14 & 15; "Form in Golf," *Outing Magazine*, April 1900, Vol. XXXVI, No. 1, pages 86–88; "The Hardest Club in Your Bag to Play," *Golf Illustrated*, January 1922, Volume 16, Issue 4, pages 16, 17, 38, & 42; "Harry Vardon on Pulling and Slicing," *The American Golfer*, July 1916, Volume 16, Issue 3, pages 175–177; "How to Become a Good Golfer," *Outing*, May 1900, Volume XXXVI, No. 2, pages 146 & 147; "Impressions of the British Open Championship," *Golf Illustrated & Outdoor America*, August 1914, Volume 1, Issue 5, page 50; "Matching the Good Player and the Bad," *Golf Illustrated*, June 1919, Volume 11, Issue 3, pages 14 & 15; "More Reflections of Harry Vardon," *The American Golfer*, December 1917, Volume 19, Issue 2, pages 320–324; "My Best Round and Some Others," *The American Golfer*, June 19, 1920, Volume 23, Issue 17, pages 11 & 22; "Noted American Golfers and Courses," *Outing Magazine*, July 1914, Issue 4, pages 466–471; "Perfect Execution with the Niblick," *Golf Illustrated*, December 1921, Volume 16, Issue 3, pages 18 & 19; "Recollections of My Early Golf, *Golf Illustrated*, June 1922, Volume 17, Issue 3, pages 16, 17, & 46; "The Reflections of Harry Vardon," *The American Golfer*, October 1917, Volume 18, Issue 6, pages 169–172; "Two Ages of Golfers," *Golf Illustrated*, July 1919, Volume 11, Issue 4, page 10; "A Vardon Dozen," *The American Golfer*, September 1916, Volume 16, Issue 5, pages 352–353; "Vardon on Links Designing," *The American Golfer*, June 1917, Volume 18, Issue 2, pages 661–665; "Vardon's Opinion of Our Golfers," *Golf Illustrated & Outdoor America*, May 1914, Volume 1, Issue 2, pages 49 & 50; "Vardon's Second Thoughts," *The American Golfer*, April 1915, Volume 13, Issue 6, pages 456–461; "Why Pros. Excel Amateurs in Iron Shots," *The American Golfer*, June 5, 1920, Volume 23, Issue 15, pages 7 & 27.

Walker, Cyril: "Correcting Your Faults, Valuable Pointers on How to Prevent Slicing," *The American Golfer*, May 17, 1921, Volume 20, Issue 9, page 14; "Recovering from Difficulties—The Chip Shot," *The American Golfer*, June 4, 1921, Volume 24, Issue 11, pages 15 & 26; "Tips on How to Play from an Uphill or Downhill Lie," *The American Golfer*, May 21, 1921, Volume 24, Issue 10, pages 12 & 29.

Wayne, Milton: "Ky Laffoon," *HK Golfer*, December 2010.

Wethered, Joyce & Roger: "The Secret of Short Mashie Approaches," *Golf Illustrated*, June 1922, pages 12 & 13; "Suggestions to cure 'Shanking'," quoted by John Duncan Dunn in "American and British Thought on Golf, I, II, III," *Golf Illustrated*, series of three articles, November 1932, page 20, and January 1933, Volume 38, Issue 4, pages 8, 9, & 41.

Worthington, H. S. "The Greatest Ten Putters," *The American Golfer*, September 23, 1922, pages 11, 26, & 27.

Wright, Ernest N.: "An Analysis of the Golf Swing," *The American Golfer*, August 1911, pp. 289–295.

Websites

Golfers who want to study the topics covered in this book more thoroughly will find the following website links helpful.

USGA Museum and Library
http://www.usga.org/history/about-museum.html

LA 84 Foundation, Sports Library and Digital Collection
http://www.la84.org/sports-library-digital-collection/

Secret in the Dirt—Putting
http://www.secretinthedirt.com/index.php/forum/32-geoff-mangum-s-book-club/289-american-golfer-magazine-on-putting

The Hickory Golf Hub—On the Shoulders of Giants
http://hickorygolfhub.com/2013/05/21/coming-soon-on-the-shoulders-of-giants/

Old Magazine Articles—Golf History
http://www.oldmagazinearticles.com/magazine-articles/golf_history

Books Cited or Recommended

Alliss, Peter (2002) *Peter Alliss' Golf Heroes*, Virgin Books, London, UK.

Armour, Tommy (1953) *How to Play Your Best Golf All the Time*, reprinted by Fireside/Simon & Schuster, New York in 1995; (1959) *A Round of Golf with Tommy Armour*, Simon & Schuster, New York; (1967) *Tommy Armour's ABC's of Golf*, Simon & Schuster, New York; (1994), *Classic Golf Tips*, Tribune Publications, Orlando, Florida. For more information on Armour, consult Charles Price, *The World of Golf: A Panorama of Six Centuries of the Game's History* (1962), and Herbert Warren Wind, *The Story of American Golf: Its Champions and Its Championships* (1956).

Boomer, Percy (1946) *On Learning Golf*, Alfred A. Knopf, New York.

Darwin, Bernard (1986) *Mostly Golf A Bernard Darwin Anthology*, edited by Peter Ryder, Ailsa, London, UK.

Dobereiner, Peter (1973) *The Glorious World of Golf*, McGraw-Hill Book Company, New York.

Duncan, George, with Bernard Darwin (1921) *Present-Day Golf*, George H. Doran Publisher, London, UK.

Duncan Dunn, John (1916) *A-B-C of Golf,* Harper and Brothers Publishers, New York & London; (1920) *Intimate Golf Talks* with Elon Jussup, Associate Editor of *Outing,* G. P. Putnam's Sons.

Dwight, James (1895) *Golf: A Handbook for Beginners,* Overman Wheel Company, New York.

Edgar, J. Douglas (1920) *The Gate to Golf,* Edgar and Company, St. Albans, England, UK.

Eubanks, Steve (2010) *To Win and Die in Dixie, The Birth of the Modern Golf Swing and the Mysterious Death of its Creator,* Ballentine Books, New York.

Frost, Mark (2002) *The Greatest Game Ever Played,* Hyperion, New York.

Hagen, Walter (1956) *The Walter Hagen Story, By The Haig Himself as Told to Margaret Seaton Heck,* Simon & Schuster, New York.

Hammond, Daryn (1920) *The Golf Swing, The Ernest Jones Method,* Chatto & Windus Publishing Co. London, UK.

Hilton, Harold (1913) *Modern Golf,* Outing Publishing Company, London, UK.

Jacobs, John (1999) *50 Greatest Golf Lessons of the Century,* with Steve Newell, HarperCollins Publishers, New York.

Jones, Ernest (1937) *Swing the Club-head,* revised edition 2003, by Skylane Publishing, Nevada.

Jones, Robert T. (1927) *Down The Fairway, The Golf Life and Play of Robert T. Jones Jnr.* With O. B. Keeler, Minton & Balch, New York; (1966) *Bobby Jones on Golf,* Broadway Books, New York; (1998) *Classic Instruction,* edited by Martin Davis, Broadway Books, New York and The American Golfer, Greenwich, Connecticut.

Keeler, O. B. (2003) *The Bobby Jones Story, The Authorized Biography,* Triumph Books, Chicago.

Leach, Henry (1914) *The Happy Golfer, Being Some Experiences, Reflections, and a Few Deductions of a Wandering Player,* MacMillan and Co., London, UK.

Longhurst, Henry (1979) *The Best of Henry Longhurst on Golf and Life*, compiled and edited by Mark Wilson with Ken Bowden, Golf Digest, Norwalk, Connecticut.

Lowe, Stephen (2000) *Sir Walter and Mr. Jones: Walter Hagen, Bobby Jones, and the Rise of American Golf*, Sleeping Bear Press, Ann Arbor, Michigan.

Mahoney, Jack (1995) *The Golf History of New England*, Weston, Massachusetts.

Matthew, Sidney L. (1999) *Bobby Jones Golf Tips, Secret of the Master*, Michigan, Sleeping Bear Press.

Morrison, Alex J. (1933) *A New Way to Better Golf*, Simon and Schuster, New York; (1934) *Pocket Guide to Better Golf*, Simon and Schuster, New York; (1940) *Better Golf Without Practice*, Simon and Schuster, New York.

Obetz, Christopher, editor (2007) *100 Classic Golf Tips*, Rizzoli International Publications, New York & Golf Digest, Norwalk, Connecticut.

Ouimet, Francis (1932) *A Game of Golf*, Houghton Mifflin Publishing; reprinted in 2004 by Edwards Brothers, Ann Arbor, Michigan.

Park, William Junior (1896) *The Game Golf*, Longmans, Green and Company, London, UK; (1920) *The Art of Putting*, J & J Gray and Company, Edinburgh, UK.

Prain, Eric Murray (1946) *Live Hands, A Key to Better Golf*, A & C Black, London, UK. Reprinted in 1998 by Warde Publishers, Portola Valley, California.

Price, Charles (1986) *A Golf Story*, Triumph Books, Chicago, Illinois.

Ross, Donald J. (1996) *Golf Has Never Failed Me: The Lost Commentaries of Legendary Golf Architect Donald J. Ross*, Sleeping Bear Press, Chelsea, Michigan.

Simpson, Bart W. G. (1892) *The Art of Golf*, David Douglas Publisher, London, UK.

Smith, Horton (1961) *The Master's Secrets of Putting* with Dawson Taylor, A.S. Barnes and Company, San Diego, California.

Taylor, John Henry (1905) *Taylor on Golf Impressions, Comments and Hints*, Hutchinson & Co., London, UK.

Thompson, Kenneth R. (1939) *The Mental Side of Golf: A Study of the Game as Practiced by Champions*, Funk & Wagnalls Co., New York, London, UK.

Tinkler, Basil Ashton (2004) *Joyce Wethered: The Great Lady of Golf*, Tempus Publishing, Oxford, UK.

Travis, Walter J. (1909) *Practical Golf*, Harper and Brothers Publishers, New York.

Vaile, P. A. (1916) *The New Golf*, E. P. Dutton and Company.

Vardon, Harry (1912) *How to Play Golf*, George W. Jacobs and Company, London, UK.

Warren-Wind, Herbert (1975) *The Story of American Golf*, Alfred A. Knopf, New York; (1985) *Following Through*, Harper Perennial, New York.

Wethered, Joyce (1933) *Golfing Memories and Methods*, Hutchinson, London, UK.

Wethered, Roger and Joyce (1922) *Golf from Two Sides*, Longmans, Green and Co., London, UK.